MYTH-BU~~~

Gulu Ezekiel is one of India's most prolific sports journalists and authors. He began his career with *The Indian Express*, Chennai, in 1982, before moving to New Delhi in 1991. His career has spanned dailies, periodicals, TV, radio and the net. Since 2001, he has been freelancing. This is his 14th sports book and the first for Rupa Publications India. He has also contributed to numerous books and annuals, as well as to over 100 publications across the world. Gulu is the author of bestselling biographies of Sachin Tendulkar, Sourav Ganguly and Mahendra Singh Dhoni.

MYTH-BUSTING

INDIAN CRICKET
BEHIND THE
HEADLINES

Gulu Ezekiel

RUPA

Published by
Rupa Publications India Pvt. Ltd 2021
7/16, Ansari Road, Daryaganj
New Delhi 110002

Sales centres:
Allahabad Bengaluru Chennai
Hyderabad Jaipur Kathmandu
Kolkata Mumbai

ISBN: 978-93-90547-17-3

First impression 2021

10 9 8 7 6 5 4 3 2 1

The moral right of the author has been asserted.

Printed at Thomson Press India Ltd., Faridabad

Dedicated to my beloved parents,
Prof Joe Ezekiel and Khorshed Wadia Ezekiel.
May their memories be a blessing.

CONTENTS

FOREWORD

Listening to stories and passing them down over generations is an integral part of Indian culture. Stories are brewed as much as cups of coffee in most households; and especially when they are about cricket and cricketers, these storytelling sessions often take on a life of their own—there is emotion, drama, curiosity, laughter...but also a fair dose of *exaggeration*! Recounted over and over again, and moulded and remoulded by enthusiastic, but not always accurate, storytellers, a lot of these distorted stories end up being treated as gospel truth.

Gulu's attempt to demystify some of these myths of Indian cricket through this book is unique and commendable. He brings together his vast journalistic experience and deep desire to sift fact from fiction, to put together a noteworthy piece of work, which while shedding much-needed light on some of Indian cricket's myths, is thoroughly engaging and entertaining. As with all of Gulu's previous works, the painstaking research that has clearly gone into the process is evident, and is the true hero of the book.

In my interactions with Gulu over the years, his love for this beautiful game has always been palpable and is evident as you leaf through the pages of this book. Underneath the facts, stories and anecdotes, lies the desire to get rid of some of these existing myths and rumours, in order to purify this beautiful game.

I am sure that the readers will enjoy and appreciate this effort. I wish the author and the book all the best.

Anil Kumble
Bengaluru, January 2021

INTRODUCTION

Why a book on Indian cricket myths?

The reasons are many. Ever since I got hooked on cricket, in India's famous summer of 1971, I have heard and read many tales surrounding the beautiful game, especially centred on Indian cricket.

It was only as I grew older and became a fulltime sports journalist, that I was able to sift fact from fiction after much reading, writing and research, and after meeting those directly involved in the tales.

For years, I have been befuddled and dismayed by these stories, but it was only with the advent of the Internet and particularly social media, that they took on a life of their own. Repeated over and over again, these stories—often painting Indian cricket and cricketers in a negative light—became accepted as fact.

Twitter, WhatsApp, Facebook, have all been carriers of fake news which spread like wildfire, and attempting to set the record straight has been a thankless task, often attracting ire and even threats, even for something as relatively innocuous as sporting history. It is my hope, therefore, that this book, drawn from multiple sources, will help to set the record straight once and for all.

The immediate inspiration for this book, however, was an article by my cricket guru, David Frith, in the December 2016 issue of *The Cricketer* monthly, headlined 'Maximum Annoyance' on the main page and 'Obnoxious Myths' in the contents section.

A nod also to the late Sir Derek Birley's brilliant book *The Willow Wand: Some Cricket Myths Explored*, though it largely deals with English cricket.

David hit out with characteristic zeal at cricket myths and stories (aka 'apocryphal tales') circulating for more than a century. Following its publication, I wrote to cricket's foremost author and historian and told him that I had been mulling a book on those lines, dealing exclusively with Indian cricket. David encouraged me to do so and provided the necessary impetus for this work. I am grateful for his support and encouragement over the decades.

In Chapter 3, I have expanded on David's irritation at commentators in the IPL referring to sixes as 'maximums'. In the article, he also mentioned an unnamed Sky TV commentator (presumably an ex-international), saying on air that a bowler was on a hat-trick in the next match after claiming two wickets in two balls and not accepting his mistake when David told him that he was wrong. For the record, a hat-trick can be claimed over two innings in a first-class/Test match but not over two matches in any format of the game.

Imagine my surprise when a reporter in a leading English national daily wrote the same after debutant Shahbaz Nadeem took the last two wickets in two balls to end the third Test versus South Africa at Ranchi in October 2019. When corrected on Twitter by me and others, he said that it was not mentioned in the Marylebone Cricket Club (MCC) laws!

My Twitter followers and cricket friends from around the world have repeatedly requested me to narrate personal anecdotes from my journalism career spanning 40 years. I have done so in a number of the chapters here while maintaining discretion where necessary, and respecting off-the-record conversations with sports personalities over the years. I trust that this will enhance the narrative.

Every book that I have written has been a team effort, this one in particular. I greatly appreciate all the help I have received from so many friends. If any of your names are missing from the acknowledgements, apologies in advance.

All the incidents, records and anecdotes in this book pertain to men's cricket, unless specifically mentioned otherwise.

For cities whose names have been changed mainly from the 1990s onwards, (Bombay/Mumbai; Madras/Chennai, etc.) I have used the original names when referring to matches and incidents that occurred before the 90s.

My special thanks to Anil Kumble for readily agreeing to write the foreword for this book.

—Gulu Ezekiel
New Delhi, January 2021
Twitter: gulu1959; website: guluezekiel.com

1

TIED UP IN KNOTS

It's a tie!

—Countless spectators and viewers

It was over an hour since cricket history had been made at the M.A. Chidambaram Stadium in Chepauk, Madras (now Chennai) on 22 September 1986, and the night shift at *The Indian Express* office on Mount Road beckoned ominously.

My day had started at 8 in the morning, leaving home in Adyar to be in time for the early start on the fifth and final day of the Test, to accommodate the 20 mandatory overs in the final hour. A scheduling snafu meant that it was the whole day at the Test and then the whole night designing the sports pages—which would be extra special that day. It's a lingering regret that I never preserved those pages.

Now, here I was, wandering the streets of Triplicane near the stadium, muttering to myself, 'It's a tie, it's a tie!' A light breeze wafted in from the Marina, slightly diffusing the terribly muggy air that surrounded Madras like a wall just before the welcome rain from the retreating or northeast monsoon in October. It's a running joke that Madras has three seasons—hot, hotter and hottest. But September was always the cruellest month.

It was only the second tied Test match in cricket history, stretching back to 1877 and 1,051 previous matches, and the first since December 1960. And 13 years later, in 1999, I found myself at Edgbaston, Birmingham, to witness the first tied match (Australia versus South Africa) in the shorter history of the 50-overs International Cricket Council (ICC) World Cup.

What makes cricket different from other sports, even unique? There are many things, but perhaps one of the most prominent though rarely spoken of, is that cricket is the only sport in the universe which can produce (in first-class/Test cricket) three distinct results: win/loss; draw AND tie—with variations in limited overs/white ball cricket where there is no provision for a draw.

And yes, in 2,393 Test matches (till the end of August 2020) there has been just one Test forfeited. That was by Pakistan to England on the penultimate day of the 2006 Oval Test after a dispute with umpire Darrell Hair, who claimed that the Pakistanis had tampered with the ball and penalized them for the alleged infringement.

In the early years of first-class cricket in India, fielding sides were known to concede matches, most notoriously when Bhausaheb B. Nimbalkar was on 443 for Maharashtra versus Kathiawar in the Ranji Trophy at Poona in 1948–49 and the fielding captain conceded (citing boredom!), with Nimbalkar within two scoring strokes of overhauling Don Bradman's then first-class world record highest score of 452.

So what differentiates a draw from a tie and why is that

even some veteran cricket followers—including players and journalists—cannot tell the difference?

Put simply, a tie is when the team batting last (fourth innings) loses all its wickets with the match totals of both sides exactly the same.

There are today 12 nations that have played Test cricket, from the first recognized Test in Melbourne in 1877 between Australia and England. In 1986, Madras followed Brisbane (1960, Test number 498: Australia versus West Indies) as just the second to end in a tie. There have been no further ties since Test number 1,052 (Madras, 1986) and number 2,393 (the third Test between England and Pakistan which ended on 25 August 2020).

In addition, two other Test matches ended with the scores level but the fourth innings incomplete (all the batsmen weren't out)—a draw, albeit equally rare.

The 1,345th Test—and the first-ever between England and Zimbabwe—at Bulawayo (December 1996) was the first to be drawn with scores tied—England needing 205 to win—on 204 for 6.

The next was Test match number 2,019, India and West Indies at Mumbai in November 2011. India, needing 243 to win, saw R. Ashwin run-out on the last ball of the match with the total reading 242 for nine—tantalizingly close to another tie, but not quite.

The whole issue of ties came into sharp focus when the ICC World Cup final between England and New Zealand on 14 July 2019 at Lord's ended with the scores level. In white ball cricket, the number of wickets lost is irrelevant—well, almost always.

This was the fifth tied game in the World Cup since it began in 1975 but the first in a final; so, for the first time in a One Day International (ODI), a Super Over was played to ensure a winner, something that had been prevalent only in T20s till then.

As the world gasped with the Super Over also being tied (England 15 for no loss; New Zealand 15 for one), England was declared the winner on the boundary count-back rule prevalent in the tournament—26 to New Zealand's 17.

Outrage followed—why wasn't the winner decided on the team losing fewer wickets (New Zealand 241 for 8, England 241 all out), why not another Super Over to decide the winner outright? Why not share the title?

The general feeling was that this was unprecedented—after all, who could possibly imagine a match going into a double-tie?

In fact, it had also happened just nine years earlier, that too in a World Cup. But it was the women's World T20 and the match between Australia and England on May 5 at Basseterre, West Indies saw both teams score 104 all out in the main match and both 6 for one wicket in the Super Over. Australia were declared winners as they had scored more sixes—one to be precise, compared to 0 by England. Again, tournament rules applied. And if the same sixes rule were to be applied in the 2019 men's World Cup? You guessed it, a tie again—both teams hit two sixes apiece in the main match!

The 2019 final was the 4,192nd ODI and the 38th to end tied and just two previous ties saw the winner decided on fewer wickets lost: India 212 for 6 in 44 overs beat Pakistan 212 for 7 at Hyderabad, India on 20 March 1987; Australia 229 for 8 in 45 overs lost to Pakistan 229 for 7 on 14 October 1988 at Lahore.

That final was followed by the Ashes and the series was deadlocked 2-2, with one draw. It was the Australians though who were celebrating—as the holders of the mythical Ashes, they retain them in the event of a drawn series, even though the tiny urn is permanently kept at Lord's.

Odd then that Australia's off spinner Nathan Lyon would be quoted as saying, 'Even though it's a 2-2 series and England is telling me I couldn't celebrate a draw, but it did exactly that during the World Cup.'

The World Cup did not end in a draw, Nathan! It was a tie—but England was then declared the winner on the boundary count-back rule.

However, following the worldwide outrage, the ICC did not waste any time in amending the Super Over rule in a tie in a knockout/final situation—the Super Over would be repeated in case it is tied too, till a winner is decided by that method.

And sure enough it happened in IPL 2020 on 18 October when Kings XI Punjab defeated Mumbai Indians via the double Super Over after the match scores and the first Super Over had both been tied.

There was also a unique tie in the history of first-class cricket in Pakistan in January 2021 when the final of the Quaid-e-Azam Trophy tournament between Central Punjab and Khyber Pakthunkwa ended tied. What was unique about it was that this was the first time in the storied history of cricket worldwide that the *final* of a first-class tournament had ended in a tie.

All T20 matches which end in ties are now decided by the Super Over but that was not always the case. The first T20 International was staged in 2004 and two years later New Zealand beat West Indies 3-0 at Auckland on 16 February 2006 by the 'bowl-out' method after the match scores were level—West Indies 126 for 7; New Zealand 126 for 8.

In the inaugural ICC World Twenty20 in September 2007, India got past Pakistan (whom they would go on to beat in the final) at Durban, winning 3-0 via the bowl-out after the scores were locked at 141, India losing nine wickets in the process and Pakistan seven. This method was now thrust into the international spotlight. And the next year, the ICC scrapped it and brought in the Super Over.

The poor Kiwis must have been sick at the thought of another Super Over. Following the World Cup final, they lost three Twenty20 Internationals (T20Is) all at home, one to England and two to India between November 2019 and January 2020 via this method.

Unlike Tests/first class, there is a provision for 'No Result' (NR) in white ball cricket, which comes into play once the toss is done but when the minimum number of overs required for a match to be considered valid is not completed. This is usually because of weather and sometimes if the pitch is deemed too dangerous to continue. This goes into the records of the two teams if the toss is done, even if not a single ball has been bowled. The shortest ODI match in terms of balls bowled was just two balls, both faced by India's K. Srikkanth (1 not out) with Kapil Dev, his opening partner, in the 1992 Benson & Hedges World Cup against Sri Lanka at Mackay on on 28 February.

A T20I also lasted two balls, in England versus New Zealand at the Oval in 2013.

There have been instances of ODIs being conceded on political/security grounds as happened first in the 1996 Wills World Cup when Australia and West Indies refused to travel to Colombo after a bomb attack in the Sri Lankan capital. Again, two matches in the 2003 ICC World Cup, in Zimbabwe and Kenya, were conceded by England and New Zealand respectively. The winner is declared by walkover and gets full points.

And while Sri Lanka felt hard done by in 1996 by the boycott, it was the Lankans who were the first country to boycott and concede a match on political grounds. That was against Israel in the 1979 ICC Trophy (which Lanka won) in England, the qualifying tournament for the Prudential World Cup the same year.

Just as Pakistan is the only country to concede a Test mid-match, India has twice lost an ODI under unusual circumstances, first against Pakistan at Sahiwal in 1978 (conceded the match due to biased umpiring) and then the 1996 Wills World Cup semifinal versus Sri Lanka at Calcutta (lost by default due to crowd disturbance disrupting the match).

The very first ODI tie (the 247th match to be played) was on 11 February 1984, between the same two teams involved in the first Test match tie, Australia and West Indies, and at the same venue (Melbourne) as the inaugural ODI in 1971, which had been between Australia and England.

This was the second final of the World Series Cup, which was based on the best-of-three match format, West Indies having won the first at Sydney, and it created a huge furore.

The West Indians raced from the field with joy when Australia's final wicket fell off the last ball of the match with the scores tied at 222. They were convinced that they had won the trophy, thus negating the need for a third decider.

But the Australian Cricket Board, after lengthy discussions, managed to persuade the sullen West Indians to be back the next day for the third final by sweetening the prize money pot. It was a farce and in protest, West Indies, which won by six wickets, did not play Viv Richards and captain Clive Lloyd; Michael Holding leading for the first time.

Under the tournament rules, if the finals were inconclusive, the team with more wins in the preliminary stage (Pakistan being the third team) would be declared the winner. West Indies were well ahead in that category but it was arranged that if Australia won the third final, the cup would be shared, in what was at the time described as a shameful manipulation of the rules, just to squeeze out a third match. Fortunately, the Aussies did not win, but the decision caused much bad blood and scathing criticism in Australian cricket circles.

There was confusion too when South Africa contrived to tie a match they should have won, with a farcical run-out that still haunts their fans, in the 1999 World Cup semifinal.

The Australians celebrated in the field but it was some time before the confused spectators were told over the PA system that Australia had gone through to the final as they had beaten South Africa by five wickets in their Super Six match four days earlier at Headingley, Leeds.

The confusion over the rules for limited-over matches (domestic games are categorized as List A which also includes ODIs, just as Test matches also come under the umbrella of first class) even saw a mistake being made in *The Hindu* daily, famed for its accuracy.

In the edition dated 22 October 2019, two quarterfinals in the Vijay Hazare (50-overs) tournament, which could not be completed due to rain, were both declared as No Result and reporter Ashwin Achal wrote as much. However, the brief scores at the end of the report listed them erroneously as draws, an obvious editing mistake for which the reporter was not responsible.

I wrote to the paper pointing out the mistake and to their credit, four days later, they published under 'Corrections and Clarifications': 'There cannot be a draw in a limited overs match. If a match is undecided, it is listed as NR (no result).'

Chepauk's Many Myths

But back to Chepauk and the many myths surrounding Tied

Test Number Two. To this day, many who witnessed the match either from the stands or on TV refer to it as a draw! One rookie journalist specializing in athletics and covering his first Test match said as much at the end—fortunately, he was corrected by those in the know and so did not bungle his report.

What has kept me amused over the years is how many present on that dramatic final day, claimed after the match, that they had predicted the result in the closing minutes.

While that can be taken with a pinch of salt, commentator Kishore Bhimani on Doordarshan was one who said so on air, as Maninder Singh took strike for the fourth ball of the final over, bowled by off spinner Greg Matthews, with the scores level. Bhimani said that two results were now possible—a win for India and a tie. Later, he admitted his mistake—a draw too was possible if Maninder survived the three remaining balls and did not score a run—which would have predated the first such draw by 10 years.

Making his 'Test debut' at *The Indian Express* was the 26-year-old Suresh Menon, most recently editor of the now-discontinued *Wisden India Almanack*. He recounted how former Bombay and Tamil Nadu batsman Sankaran Srinivasan came rushing down to the press box and shouted in his ear 'This will be a tie!' (*The Hindu*, 21 September 1986). This, after Ravi Shastri had taken two from the second ball of the final over and a single from the third, to ensure that India would not lose. I can vouch for Srinivasan's prediction, as I was sitting next to Menon.

Squatting just by the side of the press box and to my left was a volunteer from the Tamil Nadu Cricket Association (TNCA), who was blabbering hysterically even as the crowd rose to its feet in excitement. A colleague calmed him down— by slapping him.

Menon and I tried frantically to signal to our photographer at ground level below the press box to ensure he clicked the remaining three deliveries. But our voices could not be heard above the din. Indeed, all the press photographers present were blissfully unaware of the possibility of history unfolding before their eyes. Instead, they were busy getting ready for the post-match presentation ceremony, a regular tamasha at Indian grounds.

One who was aware though was Mrs Mala Mukherjee, an amateur photographer who was in the VIP section reserved for guests of the TNCA. She was running out of film and borrowed a roll from a Doordarshan cameraman just as the last few overs unfolded and, sensing something dramatic, started clicking every delivery.

A lifelong cricket fan, Mrs Mukherjee was seated on a folding wooden chair by the side of the press enclosure and had caught the eye of the media and spectators during the match, a woman photographer being rare back then. Her photograph of the moment Matthews' fifth and penultimate delivery struck last man Maninder Singh's pads and the umpire's finger shot up in a flash has been preserved for posterity and has given her a measure of lasting and well-deserved fame.

In the words of famous Australian cricket journalist Mike Coward: 'Now a celebrated, internationally renowned photographer, Mrs Mukherjee in 1986 was an enthusiastic amateur on the cusp of a professional career.'[1]

None of the professional photographers present at the ground clicked that crucial frame, though there are photos of the aftermath—the Australians racing to congratulate the bowler and the two Indian batsmen walking off in a state of shock.

---

[1]'An All-time Historic Photograph', *Between Wickets*, winter 2013.

The next morning, Mrs Mukherjee's famous photo was on the front page of *The Hindu* without a byline, though there was a byline when it was also printed in the sister publication, *Sportstar* weekly, dated 4 October 1986. It is also on the cover of the 2019 book on the 1986 tour of India featuring this famous match by Michael Sexton, *Border's Battlers: The furnace of Madras, the tied Test, a defining moment for Australian cricket.*

As with so many others, my first reaction was to leap to my feet shouting 'It's a tie, it's a tie!' I can still recall being overwhelmed with excitement at the result—the disappointment that India failed to win did not strike me at that moment.

Moments later, I turned to the Australian reporters seated behind my row and asked if any of them had witnessed the first Brisbane tie, something we in India had grown up watching in cinema halls and later on video tape. Hammering away at their typewriters and word processors, not one of those six present lifted their heads to look at me, though Alan Shiell of *News Ltd.* did manage a faint 'no'. Their focus was understandably on getting their reports through before the looming deadline, the time difference with Australia's time zones making things extra tough.

One of the recurring myths, as propagated by some of the Australian players, is that there was a discrepancy between the scorers and that Australia had in fact won the Test. This has been repeated over the years by Dean Jones—who passed away in Mumbai in September 2020 at the age of 59—as well as in the documentary, *Madras Magic: The Tied Test of '86* and also by Steve Waugh in his autobiography *Out of My Comfort Zone.*

According to Waugh, 'Meanwhile, in the scorers' booth, chaos reigned for a good half an hour, with both the ground scorers manually collating their totals after the two had different winners in their books straight after the game.'

One wonders how Waugh, celebrating on the field and in the dressing room with his mates, could know in such detail what was happening in the 'scorers' booth' after the match. I can categorically state that there was no such chaos. Jones' version is that the two scoreboards on the ground, the giant electronic one at one end of the ground and the smaller one, did not tally. Certainly, the press scorer, the late K.S. Mani, was meticulous and had it as a tie. There is also photographic evidence that the giant scoreboard showed India's total as 347 at the end of the match.

Sadly, the original scorebook is not available since the Board of Control for Cricket in India (BCCI) has never been known for its efficiency when it comes to maintaining records and preserving history.

Manager Alan Crompton in the book *The Tied Test in Madras: Controversy, Courage and Crommo* by Ronald Cardwell, had this to say:

> The crowd went crazy. For some reason I looked at my watch—it was 5.19 p.m. I along with the Australian players, Errol Alcott [the team physio] and Bob Simpson [the cricket manager/coach] ran onto the field. All of us knew it was a tie, specially the accountant in the team [reserve wicketkeeper] Greg Dyer who had been keeping a close eye on the scoreboard... Dyer in response to questions from the playing group, announced it was a tie. Simon Davis thought initially that Australia had won.

In *Great Days in Test Cricket* by Rick Smith, vice-captain David Boon claims that there was some confusion over the result and his initial reaction was that Australia had won. 'There were stories that when the sheets came back to Australia, they didn't add up and that we'd won by four runs. These sorts of things were floating around, but I don't give any pertinence to them.'

Wicketkeeper Tim Zoehrer, whose provocative antics on the final day almost led to physical confrontations with the Indian batsmen, weaves a ludicrous story in his controversial autobiography *The Gloves Are Off*. His claim that with the scores level in the final over, umpire V. Vikram Raju left the field for 10 minutes to check with the scorers is absurd. No such thing happened. No reporter present in the press box, none of the players on the field nor umpire Raju himself give any validity to Zoehrer's story and nor does the footage of the match, which includes the complete final over. In the book, Zoehrer also writes that Raju grabbed three stumps as souvenirs. This too is not borne out in the video footage. But Zoehrer certainly did not have any doubts about the tie.

The very fact that Shastri took a single from the third delivery to ensure India could not lose shows that he was aware the scores were tied. This claim by Jones and Waugh among others is not backed up in any of the reports dispatched by the Australian journalists present nor by the numerous Indian pressmen.

'Is it a draw?' asked Matthews, Jones and some others to Simpson, who had been watching from the boundary towards the closing stages and had raced onto the field. Simpson confirmed to them it was a tie. 'Is that better than a draw?' they asked incredulously. The coach said it was.

Simpson of all people should have known, for he was the only person present at Chepauk that day who had also been part of the 1960 Brisbane tie in which he had scored 92 and 0, had taken three wickets and held one catch.

That there is confusion at the end of a tied match is not unusual. It happened in the Brisbane tie as well, but this fact was not known to the cricket world at large, despite being revealed in an Indian cricket magazine by one of the umpires, Col (short for Colin) Hoy in 1978. The other umpire in the match had been Col Egar.

Hoy, who died in 1999, had revealed in the short-lived *Cricket Quarterly* (January–March 1978 issue) edited by Anandji Dossa that the West Indians thought they had won the Test when last man Ian Meckiff was run-out from the penultimate ball of the match. This though was the seventh delivery from Wes Hall as eight-ball overs were the norm in Australia back then. At Madras, it was the fifth.

Hoy gave the decision from square leg and amidst the crowd invasion and confusion, someone shouted 'It's a tie!' 'No, you mean a draw,' was the response. 'No, a tie, you bloody fool.' 'It can't be a tie.' Hoy wrote: 'A sudden air of disbelief seemed to take over. It surely was a TIE and history had been made.'

'The scoreboard had been wrong, somewhere in the last over, the attendants had missed a run, possibly the bye [from the fourth ball]. The scorers, in their excitement, had not phoned them to correct the omission.'

Hoy wrote in the article ('The hand that tied the Test') that he had not revealed this nugget of cricket history until persuaded to do so by Bharat Reddy, who had been the reserve wicketkeeper on the 1977–78 tour of Australia. Reddy told Hoy, 'One of my country's sporting papers would love to print your story.' Hoy's job with Ansett Airlines was to look after sporting groups visiting Australia and that's how he met Bishan Bedi's touring team.

The article was mailed to famed Australian statistician Charles Davis, who featured it on his website/blog, sportstats. com.au. Davis expressed surprise as this incident had not been mentioned in any of the newspaper reports or by Jack Fingleton in his book on the match, *The Greatest Test of All*. 'The reaction of the West Indies players at the end suggest that at least some of them thought they had won the Test.'

Garry Sobers in his autobiography *Sir Garry* wrote that he knew it was a tie as he always kept track of the scores but that Rohan Kanhai and others were jumping up and down thinking they had won.

Apart from the result and the fact that the final wicket fell off the penultimate ball of the match, there was not much else in common between the two famous Tests. The Brisbane Test had been the first of the series (five Tests) as was Madras (three Tests). At Brisbane, the two sides had been evenly matched till the very end; in 1986 it was Australia that was dominant right through.

A case could also be made out that only Brisbane was the perfect tie, since all 40 wickets fell. In Madras it was 32, and only 12 of those were Australian. At Brisbane, both sides scored 737 runs; in Madras it was 744—the crucial difference was the wickets that fell. Two declarations by one side in one match is indeed rare.

In fact, if not for captain Kapil Dev's barnstorming century, India would have faced the follow on. India's first innings of 397 all out—270 for 7 at close on the third day—in reply to Australia's 574 for 7 declared, meant that Border's men held all the aces. The first two days of the match were dominated by Jones' batting, even as he was wilting dangerously in the intense heat and humidity, requiring emergency hospitalization after a heroic 210.

Thrilling Tie?

The word 'thrilling' always precedes a tie in cricket. Another myth? Indeed, the match was not thrilling till Border's second declaration at the overnight 170 for 5, to set India 348 to win from 87 overs, at exactly four runs an over, on the fifth and final day. And by a remarkable coincidence, India needed four to win from the final over.

Was it a risky declaration? The players from the famous 1986 match played a reunion (one-day) match on the eve of the third and final Test between India and Australia in Chennai in March 2001. Border's explanation at the press conference, that he had declared as India were not good at chasing, raised a guffaw from Gavaskar. 'You obviously know nothing about Indian cricket history,' Gavaskar loudly proclaimed.

Gavaskar had every right to say so. At that stage, India held the world Test record for the highest winning total (406 for 4; Port of Spain 1976), highest losing total (445; Adelaide 1978), the second highest in a draw (429 for 8; Oval 1979), and at Madras in 1986, would come the record for the highest in a tie. As in 1976 and 1979, it was once again Gavaskar who inspired the chase.

The third Test in 2001, which India won in a thriller to round off a famous series, was also played in sweltering conditions with the dreaded summer just round the corner. But when I asked the eccentric Matthews, one of the heroes of the Tied Test with 10 wickets in the match, to compare the weather conditions, he shot back: 'This is like the f****** North Pole compared to 1986!'

Despite having watched every ball of the 1986 Test, it is the final day's drama that dominates my memory of the match. Such was the excitement that even the overpowering weather, that had the spectators and media gasping for breath in the stands and the players being roasted in the cauldron in the middle, was largely forgotten.

Gavaskar had etched his own place in the history books as

the first cricketer to play 100 consecutive Tests and he looked to be cruising to his 33rd century with a series of gorgeous strokes all round the wicket when he fell for 90 at 204 for three.

As Gavaskar entered the 80s, the late *Indian Express* sports editor Rajan Bala began hammering away at his trusty portable Remington. Even before he started typing, he had the headline ready, 'Gavaskar the man of destiny', so sure was he that Gavaskar would commemorate the landmark Test with a century. When he was out for 90, Bala hastily scribbled at the end of the copy: 'But it was not to be.'

Bala was in fact missing from the Chepauk press box for the first four days. Something of a cult figure in Madras cricket circles, he was on a self-imposed exile. But his great friend from his Calcutta days, Raju Mukherji, was having nothing of it. The ex-Bengal and East Zone captain was reporting the match for *Ananda Bazar Patrika* daily and *Sportsworld* weekly and persuaded Bala to turn up for the final day. It was not long before he was mobbed by his fans. 'The durbars go on as usual. Selectors, correspondents, local officials seem to need him. He tackles them as deftly as the sandwiches thrust on him', wrote Mukherji in *Sportsworld* ('Strangers Embraced', 14 October 1986).

When the mandatory 20 overs count began, India were well placed to win, with 118 runs needed and only three wickets down.

The tumble of wickets that ensued was as much due to the left-arm spin of Bright, the off spin of Matthews (the duo took five wickets apiece), the tigerish Australian fielding and Border's meticulous field placing, as it was to some panicky shots by the Indian batsmen.

So what of the dramatic denouement? Shastri has always maintained that the single he took in the final over, exposing

Maninder to three deliveries, was the right thing to do. After all, a defeat was to be avoided at all cost.

Maninder, for his part, has always maintained that he got an edge and was not out and Vikram Raju is adamant he made the right decision, even when I met him in New Delhi in December 2019. Now a sprightly 86, Raju came across as a man of firm convictions. He stressed that Maninder had always been respectful to him whenever they met.

Shastri and some of the Australians were convinced that the umpire gave his quicksilver decision as he wanted to be part of cricket history, but Raju rubbished this. He told me that as umpires they are too busy supervising the match to keep track of the scores. Hoy said the same in his article on the Brisbane tie:

> Strangely enough I did not know the scores [towards the closing stages of the Test]. All I am ever interested in is the time. When I first started umpiring it was impressed upon me by two great officials, Herb Elphinstone and George Borwick, not to worry about the runs.

The other umpire, Dara Dotiwalla, who passed away in January 2019, had all along steadfastly defended his colleague's call. Dotiwalla claimed that he did not hear the edge while standing at square leg, though with the 30,000 crowd on their feet creating an almighty din, it would have been impossible to hear anything. Dotiwalla did express relief though that he had not been at the bowler's end for that fateful final over.

In an interview for Australia's *Inside Cricket* magazine (March 2006) on the 20th anniversary of the Test, Maninder, when asked by me if he had any regrets at his dismissal, was philosophical:

Basically the regret is that we had just one run to get and if we had scored that one run, we would have won against Australia, one of the best teams in the world. But looking back now, I was part of history and people will always remember me for this. But really, I have no regrets in life.

As for the decision, he said:

Absolutely, I did nick the ball, it was an inside edge onto the pads. But then I have always maintained that since I have been an umpire myself, I have realized that it's not easy out in the middle—especially in India when the crowds are shouting at the top of their voices—it's not easy to get hold of those little nicks with all that background noise.

Whether right or wrong, it would be well nigh impossible for visiting teams and their accompanying media to complain about the bias of Indian umpiring from then on. Suresh Menon told me, 'With one raised finger, Raju raised the status of Indian umpires.' R. Mohan wrote in the *The Hindu* that it was a testament to the integrity of Indian umpires. I jokingly told Raju when we met in New Delhi that he was the world's first neutral umpire. He flashed a toothy grin.

But who was responsible for the daring second innings declaration? At the end of the match, Bala accompanied Menon to the Australian dressing room to speak to Simpson while I was told I could take a short break before the rigours of the night shift. The next morning's edition had the Bala 'exclusive' that it was Simpson's idea. This was later angrily denied by Simpson and Border to some Indian journalists. But in the *Madras Magic* documentary, Simpson indeed claims he persuaded Border to declare:

I convinced a rather reluctant Allan to close the innings at the end of that day because Allan's natural reaction would have been to go on... We know this wicket was starting to spin, we know it's going to break sometime. The odds are all in our favour. If we are gonna win this match we have to come forward and say we wanna win this match and the way to do that is to close [declare].

The last word must go to local favourite K. Srikkanth who scored 53 and 39 in front of his adoring fans.

A day after the match (as the Indian team was flying to Hyderabad for the fourth ODI), the swashbuckling opener summed things up perfectly: 'Hey guys, forget the win; we have become a part of history.'

Déjà vu Again

'It's déjà vu all over again', was one of the malapropisms that made baseball player Lawrence Peter 'Yogi' Berra famous worldwide.

It was certainly déjà vu for the Indian and Australian teams as they met in their opening match of the 1987 Reliance World Cup at the same venue just 13 months later, with seven players from both sides having been part of the playing XI in the Madras tie as well. And it was the unfortunate Maninder who once again was last man out from the penultimate ball of the match, albeit in a 50-over game.

This time it was not a tie, it was worse for the defending champions. They lost by a solitary run, the first time this had happened in a World Cup match. No doubts this time though as Steve Waugh sent the number eleven's off stump cartwheeling.

This was a winning start for the Australians, who would

ride the wave of victory to eventually emerge world champions for the first time, after beating England in the final at Calcutta.

The spotlight was on Dean Jones and Shastri again, just as in the Madras tie, but for an unusual incident that could have cost India the match. There has been much speculation over how the incident unfolded, with the late Jones often queried about it by his followers on Twitter.

Jones drove Maninder hard, fast and straight for six. Shastri, running from long off to long on, tried in vain to get a hand to it. This was the first World Cup with neutral umpires and England's Dickie Bird signaled six. Shastri though insisted it had not carried over the boundary and Bird changed his call, infuriating the Australians.

The ball dropped right below the press box and we had a perfect view as it sailed over the line. So did Hanif Mohammad, sitting in the shade of the pavilion at the boundary's edge. The famous Pakistani opening batsman was the Match Adjudicator, an early term for Match Referee, another first for the World Cup.

During one of those regular back-and-forth debates between Indian and Australian cricket fans on the subject of cheating on Twitter, someone brought up the incident, stating that Kapil Dev agreed to change the call from four to six.

Jones had responded angrily on 17 September 2017: 'Wrong! I went into the umpire's room to demand it changed! [sic] #facts #worldcup87 #Madras'.

However, in an interview to espncricinfo.com,[2] Jones credited manager Alan Crompton with the change.

Both Mike Coward in his path-breaking book *Cricket*

---

[2]Nagraj Gollapudi, 'Déjà vu at Chepauk', 5 February 2008, accessed at: https://www.thecricketmonthly.com/story/334059/d-j-vu-at-chepauk

Beyond the Bazaar: Australia on the Indian subcontinent and Michael Sexton in his book[3] also give full credit to Crompton for having the four restored to six. Here is Coward who reported both the tied Test and the Reliance World Cup for the *Sydney Morning Herald* and Australian Broadcasting Corporation:

> Convinced the ball had landed beyond the boundary by at least a metre, Crompton wasted little time in making a formal complaint to Bird and his colleague, West Indian David Archer, at the change of innings. Bird did not need much persuasion to investigate the incident and after a visit to the Indian dressing room, told Hanif Mohammad, the match adjudicator, that Indian captain Kapil Dev accepted the argument put by the Australians. The score was amended; India required 271 rather than 269 for victory.

Coward also wrote that Bird 'was careful not to accuse Shastri of any misdemeanour but at the same time voiced his concern and contempt for falling standards of sportsmanship.'

Oddly, Waugh in his autobiography *Out of My Comfort Zone*, while lauding Crompton for taking up the signal with Bird at the break, has this to say:

> Umpire 'Dickie' Bird whose initial reaction was a six, went to the Indian dressing rooms after Alan's [Crompton] inquiry, to ask Shastri, who remained noncommittal. However, when the bowler, Maninder Singh, also said he thought it was six, the umps changed our innings total from 268 to 270... This was a courageous decision by the

---

[3]Michael Sexton, *Border's Battlers: The Furnace of Madras, the Tied Test, a Defining Moment for Australian Cricket*, Affirm Press, 2019

best umpire in world cricket and a noteworthy piece of sportsmanship from Maninder.

So was it the captain Kapil Dev or the bowler Maninder who allowed the signal to be changed? Or did the batsman storm into the umpires' room? The myth lingers. When I spoke to Maninder about it, he said that he did not have a very clear recollection, 'but if a senior player and captain like Kapil-paaji agreed to the change, I would have too of course.'

What is clear though is that no action would have been taken without Crompton's intervention.

'Those were the two most important runs Alan Crompton ever scored,' remarked Border. And when the news of the revised target was conveyed to the media, Suresh Menon turned to me and said, 'Now India will lose by one run.'

Such are the ironies of the game we all love and cherish!

2

SUNNY SIDE UP

My mind snapped.

—Sunil Gavaskar on MCG 1981

Did India come close to forfeiting a Test match exactly 40 years back? Was captain Sunil Gavaskar provoked into the near-forfeit by an umpire's decision? Or was it something else? And who was it who saved the nation from the ignominy of entering the record books in a most dubious manner?

There are many myths and misconceptions floating round the dramatic events of the fourth day of the third and final Test match at the Melbourne Cricket Ground in February 1981.

India was touring Australia just two seasons after the disbanding of Kerry Packer's World Series Cricket and was part of the World Series Cup ODI tri-series with the hosts and New Zealand, apart from the three-Test series.

The first Test at Sydney saw India cave in, losing by an

innings and four runs before hanging on for a draw in the second at Adelaide. The two factors that were preying on the minds of the team and the skipper were his poor run of scores (0, 10, 23, 5, and 10 in the first innings at the Melbourne Cricket Ground [MCG]) and the umpiring which the Indians felt was heavily slanted against them.

India had conceded a big lead of 182 runs and when Gavaskar and Chetan Chauhan came out to bat in the second innings, their backs were to the wall. The deficit had almost been wiped out with the pair putting on 165 runs and Gavaskar was on 70 when the drama unfolded on the fourth morning.

Dennis Lillee struck Gavaskar on the pad, roared his appeal and umpire Rex Whitehead raised his finger. Gavaskar was livid and indicated with his raised bat that it had been bat/pad even as Lillee marched up to him and pointed to the spot where he claimed the ball had hit first. Today, the bowler would be hauled up for getting into the space of the batsman. But back then there were no match referees, let alone neutral umpires, and Whitehead's umpiring had agitated the Indians in Australia's first innings too.

Despite clear evidence in the footage to the contrary, it has always been assumed that Gavaskar pushed partner Chauhan off the field in protest against the umpire's decision.

The footage shows Gavaskar first walking off and then turning back to Chauhan and forcing him to leave the field of play. Back then, there was no live TV coverage in India, with the highlights only being shown on Doordarshan the next evening. But if one views the footage on YouTube, it is clear that something transpired between Whitehead's decision, Gavaskar's protest and his turning back to push Chauhan off the field of play.

In an interview to 'Tiger' Pataudi in the 27 April 1981 issue of *Sportsworld*, over three months after the match (the Indians travelled to New Zealand after the Australia leg), Gavaskar explained that his act had been a spontaneous one: 'My mind snapped,' he explained. There was no further explanation, save that the umpiring had been grating on the nerves of the team the whole match.

It was only in 1983, with the release of his second book *Idols,* that the picture became clear. In a chapter on Lillee, where he heaped praise on the fast bowler, Gavaskar explained:

> When the umpire did not reverse his decision, a lot of anger was boiling within me but still the idea of walking off did not strike me. When I walked past Chetan, I heard friend Lillee utter one of his profanities, which was a very delayed action from Lillee and it was then that I lost my balance and told Chetan to walk off with me.

Perhaps the two-year delay in linking the near walk-off to that verbal provocation led to the story circulating that it was the umpire's decision that was the trigger.

It was only Khalid Ansari back then who mentioned Lillee's provocation in his report of the incident in *Sportsweek* (15 February 1981), noting that Gavaskar reacted 'in disgust' after receiving a 'two-finger salute' from Lillee, after which he ordered Chauhan off the field with him.

It is now part of cricket history that manager Wing Commander Shahid Durrani raced down from the dressing room to be at the gate to prevent Chauhan from leaving the field of play—which would have resulted in a forfeit—and send next man Dilip Vengsarkar in to replace the dismissed batsman.

Bill Jacobs in his report of the match in *Australian Cricket* magazine (26 February 1981) revealed that it was Deputy Manager and former Test all-rounder 'Bapu' Nadkarni (who passed away in January 2020) who had reacted with alacrity and, sensing the danger, sent the manager racing out of the dressing room and down to the gate, hence preventing the walk-off/forfeit in the nick of time.

Lillee in his autobiography *Menace* conveniently omits his part in provoking Gavaskar, instead pouring scorn and ridicule on him for 'spitting the dummy right out of the pram.' He claims that only the batsman had doubts about the verdict, even though the TV commentators felt that there had been an edge.

'We were bemused. I was upset at times but it never changed the umpire's decision, and I never grabbed my fellow bowler and walked off the field. We had a good chuckle that someone should go to such extremes after being given out.'

Greg Chappell, the Australian captain, in his autobiography *Fierce Focus* gives the incident a slightly different angle from Lillee. He admits that Gavaskar was leaving the field after protesting the decision, 'but he turned and called poor Chauhan to come with him.'

It is pertinent to mention here that after the passing of Chauhan on 16 August 2020, all the obituaries claimed that the walk-off was in reaction to the umpire's decision. Only Gavaskar himself in his piece for PTI, published in various dailies on 17 August, pointed out: '...I lost my head after being abused by the Australians.'

In fact, there was almost a walk-off the previous day as well, initiated by wicketkeeper Syed Kirmani. Allan Border was bowled for 124 while trying to sweep Shivlal Yadav. There should have been no doubt over the dismissal, but the umpires conferred before giving Border out as they felt Kirmani may have dislodged the bails. Furious, the 'keeper told his captain that he would have walked off in protest if Border had been reprieved. Gavaskar claimed in *Idols* that this had been playing on his mind the next day and may have been subconsciously behind his own actions.

Incidentally, despite Lillee and Chappell claiming there was no doubt over the decision, Tony Greig had no doubt that it was bat/pad and wrote as much in his column in *Australian Cricket* (12 February 1981) under the headline 'Umps' mistakes riled Sunny'.

> No doubt, Indian captain Sunil Gavaskar had reached the end of his tether when he called on his opening partner, Chetan Chauhan, to join him in that third Test walk-off. Certainly, Gavaskar had 'hit the cover off the ball' and should never have been a victim to that lbw decision. At the same time, he utterly over-reacted...I feel a bit sorry for the Indians and I believe they have had the raw end of the stick this summer.

No mention was made here, though, of Lillee's verbal provocation. Gavaskar himself has always regretted his actions that day, though it was all's well that ends well, with the Indians pulling off a miracle at Melbourne when they routed Australia for 83 runs to win an amazing Test match by 59 runs and square the series.

Exactly what was spoken has never been revealed by Gavaskar, though in *SMG: A Biography of Sunil Manohar Gavaskar*, author Devendra Prabhudesai discreetly refers to the offensive word as 'a part of the female anatomy'. In 2003, Australian cricketer-turned-coach Darren Lehmann used a 'racially-motivated obscenity' (apparently pretty similar to what was uttered in 1981) in an ODI against Sri Lanka at Adelaide and was banned for five ODIs. The combination of words used in 1981 also appeared to be a mix of misogyny, obscenity and racism in one sentence and was enough to trigger the Indian captain's rage.

Till today, many Australian cricket supporters and journalists and some Indians too—despite the video evidence—continue to erroneously claim that the walk-off was prompted by the umpire's call.

It's time that myth is put to rest once and for all—just check YouTube!

Golden Year

With 2021 being the the 50th anniversary of Indian cricket's golden year (Chapter 10), it is difficult to put into words just what an impact those twin series triumphs in West Indies and England in 1971 had on the psyche of Indian cricketers and cricket fans too, so far removed from the venues and with no TV coverage.

There was no radio commentary as well from West Indies and with the time difference being what it was, one had to catch updates on All India Radio (AIR) and BBC World Service news bulletins to keep up with the dramatic events thousands of miles away.

But as news filtered back home about the batting feats of veteran Dilip Sardesai and debutant Sunil Gavaskar, it left young fans like me spellbound and awestruck. For the older generations, there was a sense of wonder, considering the tragedy and trauma of the earlier tour of 1962 which had left a deep scar on Indian cricket (see Chapter 9).

'Glory be, Gavaskar' was the headline on the cover of *Sportsweek* (25 April 1971), above a photo of the fresh-faced opening batsman who had stunned the cricket world with a century and a double century in the fifth and final Test at Port-of-Spain, Trinidad. The draw meant that India had won the series 1-0 against the might of Garry Sobers' men, holding on to the victory at the same venue in the second Test match.

Gavaskar made his debut in the second Test with twin 60s, remaining unbeaten in the second, as he hit the winning runs. Never before had India beaten West Indies—and here it was happening on their own soil—in 24 previous Test matches. In 1962, India had suffered the ignominy of a 5-0 whitewash.

It was Sardesai who set the ball rolling in the first Test at Kingston, Jamaica, with the first Test double century by an Indian abroad. His three centuries at the average of 80.25 was an outstanding effort, especially as he was one of those who had suffered much trauma on the previous tour.

But he was overshadowed by the record-breaking feats of Bombay teammate Gavaskar, whose 774 runs in four Tests, with an average of 154.80 with four centuries and three fifties in his eight innings, established a new world record for highest aggregate in a debut Test series. Together, they scored more than half of India's runs in the entire series. The previous best on debut had been by West Indies' George Headley with 703 versus England in 1929–30. Gavaskar's record has been unchallenged after five decades and also remains the highest aggregate by an Indian in a Test series. It is the second highest aggregate for a player playing four Tests in a series and remarkably in the 2019 Ashes, Australia's Steve Smith scored the same—774 runs at 110.57 and also in four Tests.

Now, traditional fast bowling—lightning fast and with bouncers galore—has been the forte of West Indies cricket. So, how ferocious and frightening was the bowling that Gavaskar and company faced, as has been repeatedly stated over the years? Let us explore that myth in detail.

But first, it is amusing to read famed *The Times of India* cricket correspondent K.N. Prabhu write in the February 1971 issue of *The Cricketer* (UK) that after 'a remarkable sequence of centuries in the domestic season, Gavaskar has all the makings of an opener, but he is a slack fielder and it may be difficult to fit him into a team that distinguished itself by its close-in fielding in the last series against Australia.'

Apart from his batting records—first to reach 10,000 Test runs, first to cross Don Bradman's 29 centuries—Gavaskar also became the first Indian to take 100 catches!

West Indies cricket was going through a slump that lasted from 1968 to 1972, during which they did not win a single series under the captaincy of Sobers. While the batting, boasting of the great man himself, Rohan Kanhai, Clive Lloyd, Roy Fredericks and Charlie Davis, was formidable, it was in the bowling department that the home side suffered.

The feared opening bowling attack of Wes Hall and Charlie Griffith was finished with Test cricket and leading off spinner Lance Gibbs was out of form.

The pace bowling attack consisted of three bowlers coming back into the side after nearly two years—John Shepherd (who played two Tests in the series), Grayson Shillingford and Vanburn Holder, both of whom played in three Tests. In addition, there were two debutants in Uton Dowe (two Tests) and Keith Boyce (one). By the end of their careers, all the five bowlers would have played a total of 77 Tests, with Holder (40) and Boyce (21) constituting the bulk.

Remarkably for a series in West Indies, it was an off spinner, Jack Noreiga, who headed the bowling averages and had most wickets (17), with nine of these coming in a solitary innings in the second Test, which India won by seven wickets, the only result in the five Tests. He bowled the most deliveries too (1,322) but just eight behind was skipper Sobers with 12 wickets, some with pace and some with spin.

Not Quite So Frightening

Repeated references to this series on social media and elsewhere highlight Gavaskar's awesome batting and the 'frightening West Indies bowling attack'. None of the bowlers in that 1971 series could be categorized as frightening by any stretch of the imagination, certainly not in the grand tradition of West Indies fast men, and surely even Gavaskar would agree on this point.

In the book *The Innings of My Life*, he told the compiler Jack Bannister: 'The hundreds against the West Indies beforehand [before the 1971 England tour] were on good pitches against a reasonable attack, but with no outright pace. I have always felt that batting against genuinely quick bowling is the supreme examination of a batsman.'

In an interview to Sunder Rajan in his book *India vs West Indies 1971* captain Ajit Wadekar had this to say about the Windies' bowling:

> Holder, perhaps, was their best. He was a little slower than [Wes] Hall but moved the ball both ways. He will turn out to be another Hall. Shillingford and Boyce were quite quick. Youthful Dowe was really quick, but inexperienced. Shepherd was the shrewdest of the lot. He moves and cuts the ball both ways, sizes up the batsmen properly and bowls to his field. His bouncers were the most difficult to handle.

Shepherd became a legend in English county cricket for Kent, but his Test career consisted of five Tests for just 19 wickets. Holder had 109 in his 40 Tests but never bowled above fast-medium and was certainly not a patch on Hall, as Wadekar had predicted.

Myths do have a tendency to go viral on social media,

but imagine a West Indian cricket legend making the same observation!

Former captain and 'rebel' Alvin Kallicharran in his book *Colour Blind: Struggles, Sacrifice and Success of the Cricket Legend* has this to say about the famous series: 'Sunny [Sunil Gavaskar] who was brought up on the Indian tracks that assisted spin, instantly adapted to make heaps of runs on the much quicker West Indian pitches against *frightening* [emphasis mine] pacemen in his first series and was nothing short of sensational.'

Sobers, however, in his autobiography lamented, 'With Hall and Griffith retired, we boasted no true pace and India's win in the second Test in Trinidad was enough, as the other four Tests were drawn.'

In his *A History of West Indies Cricket*, the former Jamaican Prime Minister Michael Manley wrote: 'Following the retirement of Hall and Griffith, West Indies had no real pace attack. Vanburn Holder of Barbados was, at best, fast medium. Jamaica's Uton Dowe was quicker, but not really top-class, while Grayson Shillingford of Dominica was equally below Test standard.'

In fact, *Wisden Cricketers' Almanack* (1972) remarked: 'Sobers when roused, looked the most dangerous.'

Dowe had one fiery spell in the fourth Test at Bridgetown, Barbados where he picked up four wickets in the first innings including Gavaskar (1), for his only failure of the series, to reduce India to 70 for 6 in reply to West Indies' 501 for five declared. But that was it and India wriggled out of that tight spot. The pacers did send down bouncers galore in the series but their speed never posed any real danger. Sobers said of Dowe, 'He thought he was another Roy Gilchrist, but he didn't have Gillie's pace and accuracy...he tried to bounce everyone.'

In fact, Dowe could be said to be the only cricketer to be laughed out of Test cricket. The incident occurred in the first Test against Australia at his hometown of Kingston in February 1973 where he was being hammered to all parts of the ground by opener Keith Stackpole.

Suddenly a wag from the crowd yelled out to captain Rohan Kanhai, 'Hey Kanhai, remember the eleventh commandment!' Slight pause. 'Dowe shall not bowl!'

The crowd roared, the players chuckled, and that was the end of Dowe's brief international career.

Nothing can or should take away from the achievements of Gavaskar, Sardesai and company. But 'frightening' bowling? Surely not. This was a brief period in West Indies cricket history when their fast bowling attack was at its weakest following the end of the Hall and Griffith era. That fearsome tradition though would be restored by 1976.

The Helmet Story

Test cricket had been played for 100 years before batsmen thought it prudent to protect their skulls from the rock-hard ball hurled at lightning speed by testosterone-pumped fast bowlers.

It took a broken jaw, suffered by Australia's David Hookes at the hands of West Indies's Andy Roberts at the Sydney Showground, within a month of Kerry Packer's breakaway World Series Cricket (WSC) in December 1977, to send batsmen into a panic.

WSC was all about attacking batting and speed, with a virtual conveyor belt of the world's quickest and most dangerous bowlers pounding away, and Packer saw helmets as a sort of insurance policy. He insisted that his employees, the cream of the world's cricketers, protect their heads and thereby his own commercial interest. It was England opener Dennis Amiss who thus became the first cricketer to wear one, a modified motorcycle helmet. Others followed in a hurry. And in March 1978 at Bridgetown, Barbados, it was Australia's Graham Yallop who entered the history books when he wore a helmet in a Test match for the first time. The crowd hooted and mocked him, but there would be no turning back.

The early helmets were bulky, uncomfortable and made communications between the batsmen difficult. Yallop made the mistake of discarding it for the next match against Guyana, who had the fearsome Colin Croft in their ranks. Big mistake— Croft broke his jaw!

Even with helmets, batsmen (and fielders) have suffered serious injuries, culminating in the tragic loss of Philip Hughes' life in a Sheffield Shield match at Sydney in November 2014. There have been modifications in both equipment and Laws since.

Folklore has it that the only two batsmen in that era who never wore a helmet were Sunil Gavaskar and West Indies legend Vivian Richards. Myth or reality?

Well, Gavaskar, from late 1983 till 1987, the final year of his career, did wear a specially manufactured fibreglass skull cap which he placed under his floppy sun hat.

The inspiration came from Mike Brearley, who wore something similar in the home Ashes series against Australia in 1977, before switching to a conventional helmet the next year. Brearley said that he had it designed in consultation with Tony Greig, following the home series the previous year against West Indies with the fearsome fast bowling armada of Michael Holding, Andy Roberts and Wayne Daniel, who were liberal with bouncers.

Before that, in 1933 at Lord's, England's 'Patsy' Hendren caused considerable mirth and outrage when he came out to bat against the fiery pace of West Indians Manny Martindale and Learie Constantine with a similar contraption made by his wife. Way back in 1870, Nottinghamshire's George Summers had been struck on the head at Lord's by MCC fast bowler John Platts and had died four days later. The next batsman, Richard Daft came in with a towel swathed round his head in protest against what he considered dangerous bowling. The Lord's pitch was considered poor back then and the tragedy led to efforts to improve it.

Douglas Jardine, the father of 'bodyline', must have got the shock of his life when he toured the land of his birth with the first official English team to visit India in 1933–34. The famed Indian fast bowling pair of Mohammad Nissar and L. Amar Singh, with Amar's elder brother L. Ramji (Chapter 6) posed grave physical danger to the English batsmen. Jardine ordered all this batsmen, including himself, to wear the sola topi or pith hat, made of strong but lightweight material, which was favoured by Europeans in the tropics, to protect them from the harsh sun. It was just as well, as opener Fred Bakewell received a blow to his head from Nissar at Patiala, which crushed his topi but probably saved his life.

The Indians wore this hat too when they toured Australia in 1947–48 under the captaincy of Lala Amarnath. And it was Lala's middle son Mohinder who was the last to wear it in a Test match against Australia at Bombay in November 1979. It was not of much help though, as he fell on his stumps evading a bouncer from Rodney Hogg and was out hit wicket for 2. The hat was never seen again in a major cricket match.

Gavaskar in his book *Runs 'n Ruins* wrote that he had the skull cap designed in England in 1980 when he was playing county cricket for Somerset. The manufacturer in Nottingham measured his head and made a mould of it from dental clay and from that mould made the skull cap with necessary modifications. He had avoided wearing a helmet as he suffered from a stiff neck and the added weight would have caused him problems, he claimed.

For three years, the skull cap remained unused in his kit bag as he travelled the cricket world. It was only after being struck on the temple by Malcolm Marshall in the third Test at Georgetown, Guyana, in April 1983 (while scoring 147 not out), that he decided it was time to wear it.

It was his good friend Imran Khan who had urged Gavaskar to wear some sort of skull cap during the tour of Pakistan that preceded the West Indies tour.

Gavaskar did not wear it during the triumphant Prudential World Cup in England and the first time he used it in an international series was when Pakistan toured India just three months after the World Cup. The skull cap's international debut came in the first ODI at the Lal Bahadur Shastri Stadium, Hyderabad, on 10 September 1983 and was worn in the three Test matches that followed, as well as during the subsequent West Indies home series.

In a photo of Gavaskar batting, with it peeping out from below his sunhat, which appeared in *Sportstar* (24 September 1983*)* from the first Test at Bangalore versus Pakistan, the caption erroneously refers to it as a 'steel skull cap'.

However, that was not actually the first match appearance of the famous headgear. In an interview to Lokendra Pratap Sahi of *The Telegraph*, Kolkata (9 January 2018) in Cape Town, he confessed that he was not quite sure when he first wore it.

Q: I can't recall the match when your skull cap made its debut...

A: Actually, I cannot either... Would have been the home series against Pakistan, at the start of the 1983–84 season, or the first Test (in Kanpur) against the West Indies later that season.

In fact, the debut was made during the Platinum Jubilee of the Buchi Babu Invitation Tournament held in Madras in August 1983, where he was representing his office team Nirlons in the traditional (back then) curtain raiser to the season.

The tournament was memorable, as it was the first time that the 1983 World Cup stars were being seen in action, just two months after the triumph at Lord's. All the Bombay players—Gavaskar, Ravi Shastri, Balwinder Singh Sandhu and Sandeep Patil—were representing their corporate teams and the weeklong tournament attracted huge crowds at the M.A. Chidambaram Stadium. It was memorable for me on a personal level too, as it marked my first year in the profession and I reported the tournament for *The Indian Express*.

But I had my doubts over whether Gavaskar had unveiled the skull cap during the tournament, as I had not mentioned it in any of my reports which I went back and checked. I then found a photo which provided proof in *Sportstar*, dated 10 September 1983. The caption read: 'Gavaskar tried on a Brearley-style skull cap for a while. Time for a helmet against the West Indies?' West Indies, yes. But first came Pakistan in September.

It was also at Madras that Gavaskar decided to pull the hook shot out of cold storage. He had resisted using it post his debut series in West Indies in 1971, feeling that it was not a percentage shot. But with Marshall, Holding and company bringing their armoury to India, he had a change of heart. From now on he would fight fire with fire and after the trauma of the first Test at Kanpur, where Marshall ran amok, Gavaskar employed the hook to devastating effect in his century in the second Test at New Delhi and through the rest of the series, which ended at Madras with his highest Test score of 236 not out.

In the semifinal for Nirlons against TNCA President's XI, Gavaskar unveiled his new attacking avatar. His century contained nine sixes and 12 fours, racing from 100 to 174 in a mere 23 balls. The ecstatic fans at Chepauk could scarcely believe their eyes and neither could this rookie reporter who had a perfect view from the Madras Cricket Club pavilion.

Postscript

That skull cap may have emboldened him to go for his shots, but it could also have proven fatal, as he told Gaurav Kapoor on his show *Breakfast with Champions* in 2019. After his final first-class match, the 1987 Bicentenary 'Test' at Lord's, Gavaskar presented the skull cap to the Lord's museum, deciding that he did not need it for the Reliance World Cup in India later that year. It turns out that a German neurologist who happened to visit the museum saw it and opined that whoever was wearing it would have been killed instantly on impact if the ball had struck it!

So what about Vivian Richards, aka Master Blaster, a batsman by style and temperament who could not have been more different from the Indian master?

While Gavaskar always put up a pragmatic front for not wearing a helmet, Richards was more macho and patriotic in his justification.

He told PTI in an interview that was widely published in the Indian media on 8 May 2013:

> At that time, I thought it (representing West Indies) was the highest honour that would be bestowed upon any individual. I don't think I would have done that cap any justice, if I had anything else on the head. I felt that proud wearing that cap...I felt God will protect me from whatever I was facing out in the middle.

Richards doubled down on that sentiment in a podcast with Shane Watson in April 2020. 'The passion for the game I felt was such that I wouldn't mind dying playing something that I love. If this is what I chose [not wearing a helmet] and I go down here, what better way is there to go?'

Circumstantial evidence however points towards Richards having worn a helmet during his storied career, albeit briefly. The first occasion was reportedly during Kerry Packer's World Series Cricket, which ran for two seasons from 1977–78 to 1978–79 and in which, as written earlier, the world's fastest were dishing it out in spades.

Yes, Richards had the advantage of not facing his own battery of pacemen, at least in international cricket. But in WSC, there was Australia's Dennis Lillee, Jeff Thomson and Len Pascoe, Pakistan's Imran Khan and South Africa's Garth Le Roux and Mike Procter, all of whom made the batsmen their targets.

The topic comes up every now and then on Twitter and a couple of collectors have claimed that they have video footage of Richards in a helmet, though it has never been uploaded. Some others have claimed to have seen photos of the same. But after extensive research, the only one I could find was of Richards wearing a helmet in the nets during the second season of WSC (1978–79). The photo was published in the 1997 book *200 Seasons of Australian Cricket.*

It is possible that he took the call after receiving a head injury (while wearing a cap), from a bouncer from, of all bowlers, Greg Chappell, which needed on-field attention. This happened on 15 January 1978 while playing for the WSC World XI against WSC Australia at the Sydney Showground in the fourth of the WSC's 'Supertests', while scoring 119. This is how the incident was described in the book *Cricket Alive! World Series Cricket: The First Exciting Year.*

> Who was to predict, least of all Viv Richards himself, that when on 74, that impeccable timing was going to falter by one split fraction of a second. For it was then, while trying to hook a ball from Greg Chappell, that Richards missed. The ball struck him on the forehead, and knocked him down. It was only after treatment with icepacks that he was able to resume.

Further, in an interview to thecricketmonthly.com (3 November 2016),[4] England and Surrey off spinner Pat Pocock had this to say:

> Sylvester Clarke [of Barbados, West Indies and Surrey] was the most feared man in world cricket. Richards went into print saying he didn't like facing him. Viv says he didn't wear a helmet. He bloody did: he wore one twice against Surrey when Clarke was playing. Fearsome, fearsome bowler. I played against Roberts, (Michael) Holding, (Wayne) Daniel, (Joel) Garner,

---

[4]Scott Oliver, 'The wrist is a forgotten area of spin bowling' accessed at http://www.espn.com/cricket/story/_/id/17959579/former-england-offspinner-pat-pocock-looks-back-career

Marshall, (Patrick) Patterson, (Courtney) Walsh, (Curtley) Ambrose—all of them. I faced Sylvs in the nets on an underprepared wicket, no sightscreen, no one to stop him overstepping. There was no one as fearsome as Clarkey was. And everybody knew it.

As per my research, one of the occasions was possibly at the County Ground, Taunton on 16, 18 and 19 August 1986. It was an unusual match—rain washed out play on the second day, the 18th. On the 17th, the teams played a 40-over match in the John Player Special League (also ruined by rain) which was the practice back then.

Somerset, in reply to Surrey's 427 for nine declared, closed their innings at 83 for no loss on the final morning after adding 49 runs to their overnight total (461 runs in all were scored on the first day) and as per prior understanding between captains Pocock and Peter Roebuck, Surrey forfeited their second innings, leaving Somerset a target of 345. They collapsed to 166, with Clarke claiming 5 for 31, including a fierce opening burst of 3 for 2 from 11 deliveries, including Richards (who did not bat in the first innings), bowled for 7. 'Richards lost his off stump to a shot of unimpressive application,' David Foot wrote in *The Guardian* (20 August 1986).

This was the final season for Richards (and Joel Garner) before their highly controversial sacking at the end of the season and there was a cloud over both of them by this time in the season. Roebuck in his autobiography *Sometimes I Forgot to Laugh* gives a pointer to Richards' state of mind. 'Viv had been persuaded to accept the vice-captaincy but was not prepared to bat at one-wicket down [he batted at number four in the Surrey match], saying he was "done with all that bravery ignorance thing".'

It is well known that whenever Richards came across his West Indian teammates in domestic matches, whether in England, West Indies or elsewhere, those fearsome fast men would put in an extra effort for speed and intimidation. And Richards, it seems, was their favourite target.

It's not altogether surprising then that in the Shell Shield and Red Stripe Cup in the Caribbean (representing first Combined Island, then Leeward Island), the first-class batting average of Richards is an unimpressive 39.17 (46 matches; 78 innings; 4 not out; 2,899 runs; HS: 168 not out; 9 hundreds; 14 fifties) against his career first-class average of 49.40 (114 centuries in 796 innings) and Test average of 50.23 (26 centuries in 182 innings). It should also be noted that Richards did not have to face the express bowling of Andy Roberts, Eldine Baptiste, Curtly Ambrose and Winston Benjamin since they played in the same domestic side. And against the most formidable fast bowling sides, Barbados and Jamaica, he had just one century in 23 innings (27.32 average) and three from 20 (34.79) respectively.

Indeed, Richards has gone on record stating that Clarke (who died in 1999 aged 44) was the only fast bowler he felt 'uncomfortable' facing. Those who did face him, have some hair-raising tales to tell, and some even now carry the scars, physical and mental, such was Clarke's terrifying speed and hostility.

In late 2019, Indian captain Virat Kohli made the statement that coach, former captain (for one Test) and all-rounder Ravi Shastri did not wear a helmet while opening the batting, which he did in 26 innings in Test matches and 49 in ODIs. This is incorrect. Shastri, like almost all his teammates and cricketers around the world, wore a helmet throughout his international career.

3

LAGAAN AND CRICKET'S SIX APPEAL

That's a [sponsor's name] Maximum!

—Various Indian Premier League (IPL) commentators

At the outset, I would like to clarify that this chapter does not deal with minor matches where there have been numerous freak incidents which cannot always be independently verified and where the standard of the bowling is often very weak.

When the cricket-themed film *Lagaan: Once Upon a Time in India* was released in 2001, it created a sensation with its feel-good story of a bunch of poor farmers taking on the might of the British Raj in a winner-takes-it-all cricket match.

Directed by Ashutosh Gowariker and with producer Aamir Khan in the role of Bhuvan, the leader of the villagers and captain of the team, it became only the third Indian film to be nominated in the Best Foreign Film section at the 2002 Oscars. Though it did not win, it did sweep all national awards and became a blockbuster that created a positive vibe across the country with its feel-good and patriotic message.

In the climactic scene, Bhuvan attempts to win the match with a last-ball six, only for the villainous Captain Andrew Russell (played by British actor Paul Blackthorne) to take the catch. But in doing so, his foot crosses the boundary line and the umpire signals a six. The Indians thus win a thrilling match and are exempted from paying cess ('lagaan' in Hindi) on their farms for the next three years.

Like many sports-based films and TV shows, including multiple Oscar-winner *Chariots of Fire* and the Australian TV serial *Bodyline*, *Lagaan* took advantage of so-called artistic license to play fast and loose with the history of the game.

Lagaan begins by stating that the story is set in 1893 in Champaner village in the erstwhile Central Provinces, where the farmers are suffering after three years of drought and find the burden of taxation imposed by the British too much to bear.

The year is important in cricket history, as till 1910 a hit crossing the boundary line was counted as four—as was a shot across the ground—and not six. In Australia, though, it counted as five and the batsman lost the strike. For a six to be recorded, the ball had to clear the stadium altogether—an extremely rare occurrence, given the size of the stadia. That changed in England from 1911 onwards. In Australia, it was changed in the 1904–05 season.

Of course in *Lagaan*, the match was played on a maidan or open field. But even then, the catch would have counted as a dismissal, as it was only from 1968 onwards that the Laws were changed. Till then, a catch was legal even if the fielder crossed the boundary line after he had caught the ball.

In recent years, with the advent of acrobatic catches on the boundary, a fielder is allowed to parry the ball, cross the boundary and jump back into the field of play to complete the catch—or else allow a teammate to complete it.

Sobers the First

In 1968, the very first year the Law had been changed, it was the prince of all-rounders, West Indian legend Garry (later Sir Garfield) Sobers, playing in his first year in county cricket, who carved his name in the history books by becoming the first to hit six sixes in an over in professional cricket.

Playing for Nottinghamshire against Glamorgan at the St Helen's ground, Swansea on Saturday 31 August, Sobers smashed left-arm spin bowler Malcolm Nash for 36 runs in the over. Nash was a medium pacer, but impressed by the success of Test bowler Derek Underwood, he decided to try his hand at spin. Sobers ended that particular experiment.

It was the first day of the final match of the season and captain Sobers was looking for quick runs and a declaration when he reached the crease with the total at 308 for five. Sobers had sent in John Parkin at his usual No. 6 position, as he had been held up at the local bookies, placing a bet on the horses.

It happened to be the 28th and final match of Parkin's brief first-class career and he was a mute spectator at the non-striker's end while Sobers went about his mayhem. 'There I was, a solid and reliable cricketer, basically just holding up my end while Sobers, a brilliant player, was making history,' is how Parkin recalled the feat in an article in the magazine *Back Spin* (summer 2012).

Nash, who died at the age of 74 in 2019, was no pushover, with close to 1,000 first-class wickets over 17 years for Glamorgan. But though he never played international cricket, his name is also in the history books, something that he never regretted. Indeed, much to Sobers' annoyance, Nash made a tidy packet recounting the story countless times on the cricket after-dinner circuit in England, where he was a much sought-after guest.

In fact, even as they were leaving the field at the end of the day to be interviewed, Sobers spotted Nash smiling to himself. 'I asked him what he was smiling about,' wrote Sobers in his autobiography. 'I want you to understand that I'm with you,' Nash replied. 'I don't mind that I'm at the wrong end, I'm in the record books with you.'

Remarkably, BBC Wales had their TV crew at the ground and that historic feat is there for all to see. And it's been watched over a million times on YouTube!

In the commentary box was the patriarch of Welsh cricket, Wilf Wooller. He had been asked by his producer to hand back to the studio at the start of the famous over but, fortunately for one and all, including the chastened producer, Wooller refused to do so.

It was the new Law introduced that very year, which allowed Sobers to complete the feat. The fifth ball was not quite middled and fielder Roger Davis at long off back-pedaled furiously before clasping the ball, only to tumble over the boundary. Sobers, thinking he was out, began the walk. But the partisan Welsh crowd was thoroughly enjoying the carnage and urged him to stay. Umpires Eddie Phillipson and John Langridge conferred, perhaps verifying the change, and Phillipson then signaled the six.

Nash could have bowled a deliberate wide or no ball to spoil it, but instead he bowled a quicker ball and Sobers deposited it outside the ground and onto the adjoining road. In 1977 at the same ground, Nash was at the receiving end again as Lancashire's Frank Hayes hit five sixes and 34 runs in one over off his bowling, the second ball going for four.

Fast forward to the 2019 ICC World Cup final at Lord's. England need 22 from 9 balls with three wickets in hand to overhaul New Zealand's 241. Ben Stokes smashes Jimmy Neesham to the midwicket boundary where Trent Boult is waiting. But as he relays the ball to Martin Guptill, Boult's foot touches the ad boards and it's signalled a six—126 years after Captain Russell and *Lagaan*!

How England won the title after a double tie (see Chapter 1) is now part of cricket history.

It was a story of redemption for Stokes who had been left shellshocked after the final of the ICC World T20 against West Indies at Kolkata in 2016. Defending a healthy 19 runs in the final over of the match, Stokes was smashed for four consecutive sixes by Carlos Brathwaite from his first four deliveries.

Remarkably, Stokes was in the thick of it again, less than six weeks after the World Cup final, with a sensational innings of 135 not out in the fourth Ashes Test at Leeds, which kept England's hopes alive in the series, with some audacious strokes that saw him hit eight sixes. The Test record is held by Pakistan's Wasim Akram with 12.

The advent of the T20 format in England in 2004 and the birth of the Indian Premier League four years later saw six-hitting reach unreal proportions, nearly reducing bowlers to cannon fodder.

Batsman's Game

Cricket has always been a batsman's game but now more than ever, particularly in white ball cricket. Pitches have been made to suit batsmen, boundaries have been brought in till they resemble a school cricket match and technology has seen the bat assume massive proportions while at the same time not increasing the weight by much. And for some years now, two white balls per innings, fielding restrictions and Powerplays have all made the game one-dimensional, forcing bowlers around the world to innovate. The 'free-hit' too allows the batsman the luxury of going for the big hit without the risk of being dismissed.

In fact, Clive Lloyd, Graeme Pollock, Sachin Tendulkar and a few others used bats that were heavier than the modern wonders and weighed upto three pounds. The difference is that the 'sweet spot' and edges have been enlarged to such an extent that top and bottom edges now routinely sail over the tiny boundaries for so-called 'maximums'. Modern manufacturing methods have allowed moisture content in the willow to be reduced, making bats lighter while increasing their power. They do have bigger edges and greater depth even today, though the dimensions have now been standardized so that some of the monsters of the mid-2000s have been effectively outlawed.

There was a conversation between Harsha Bhogle and Sunil Gavaskar during the ODI against West Indies at Visakhapatnam on 18 December 2019, which was an eye-opener. Even as another six was sent soaring over the boundary, Bhogle asked Gavaskar: 'What would your generation have given for shots that go for six off the toe-end of the bat?' To which Gavaskar promptly replied: 'What would my generation have given for such ridiculously short boundaries?'

Remember, the one and only Don Bradman hit just 45 sixes in his entire first-class career of 28,067 runs inclusive of six sixes in his Test total of 6,996.

Following Sobers' landmark, in January 1985 in the Ranji Trophy match for Bombay versus Baroda at Wankhede Stadium, Bombay, Ravi Shastri emulated the feat off bowler

Tilak Raj. But it was not till the 2007 ICC World Cup match at Warner Park, Basseterre, St Kitts, that this was achieved in an international match.

South Africa's Herschelle Gibbs gave the treatment to the hapless Daan van Bunge of the Netherlands. Barely six months later, it was India's Yuvraj Singh who lit up the inaugural ICC World T20, with England's Stuart Broad at the receiving end at Durban.

Since then, Worcestershire's Ross Whiteley against Yorkshire (bowler Karl Carver) in the NatWest T20 Blast at Headingley in 2017 and Afghanistan's Hazratullah Zazai for Kabul Zwanan against Balkh Legends (bowler Abdullah Mazari) in the Afghanistan Premier League at Sharjah in 2018, have followed in their footsteps. And on 5 January 2020, it was the turn of Leo Carter in New Zealand's domestic T20 Super Smash, who made it a group of 7 for Canterbury versus Northern Districts at Christchurch, the bowler being Anton Devcich.

Remarkably, save for Shastri and Gibbs, all the batsmen were left-handers. Of the seven bowlers at the receiving end, all were spinners—save for Broad; five of the six were left-armers, leg spinner van Bunge the only exception. And except for Shastri's innings (black and white photos being the only evidence), the others were all televised.

In the 1979 county championship, South Africa's Mike Procter also smashed six consecutive sixes for Gloucestershire versus Somerset at Taunton, but these were not in one over. Alex Hales did the same in the T20 Blast in 2015.

Among the kings of six-hitting in the modern era, it is New Zealand's Brendon McCullum, England's Alex Hales and Eoin Morgan (who holds the ODI record with 17), West Indians Chris Gayle, Andre Russell and Kieron Pollard, Australia's Chris

Lynn and Aaron Finch and India's Rohit Sharma and M.S. Dhoni who stand out. Pollard, who has represented 30 teams, has in fact hit more sixes than fours (647 to 643) in his 496 T20 games till the end of 2019. In March 2020 he became the first to appear in 500 T20 matches.

Gayle, with his stand-and-deliver style of power-hitting, called his 2016 autobiography 'Six Machine: I Don't Like Cricket...I Love It'. A bit of advice on the back cover, for those whose car windscreens he had smashed, asked them to park their cars 'further away from the ground next time the Six Machine comes to town. It's worth the walk.' He holds the record for most sixes in international cricket (Tests, ODIs, T20I) with 534 from 530 innings. Next best and way behind is Pakistan's Shahid Afridi with 476 from 508. Rohit Sharma is third with 410 from 363 (till the end of 2019).

The most runs in one over in T20s is 37 by both Gayle and Zazai. Including one no-ball/free hit, the one over from Prasanth Parameswaran (Kochi Tuskers Kerala) went for 37 in the IPL 2011 match at Bengaluru, with four sixes and three fours being struck by Gayle for Royal Challengers Bangalore. The no-ball was hit for six and the free-hit for four. In the case of Zazai, the extra run came from a wide.

Maximum Mayhem

So what about the 'maximums' from one ball? David Frith, writing in the December 2016 issue of *The Cricketer* ('Maximum Annoyance', see Introduction) expressed his irritation at commentators claiming a six is a 'maximum'. 'It is ignorant (and cash-crazy) IPL commentary speak. It is also wrong. Six is not the most runs from one ball. There have been sevens, eights and nines.' And also a 10 by Wood, as explained later in this chapter, though that was a one-off.

Believe it or not, a batsman ran all nine (without overthrows) in a match in 1842. It was not till the 1860s in England that boundaries were demarcated by ropes and even spectators' tents. Before that, batsmen could keep running while fielders chased after the ball even as it crossed the ground.

Hence, at Parker's Piece, Cambridge, to quote Arthur Haygarths' *Scores and Biographies*, Frederick Ponsonby batting for MCC versus Cambridge University 'made a hit to leg for 9, being one of the longest recorded in any match where there was no overthrow' and it was also noted that 'the fieldsmen to throw the ball up were young and active', presumably meaning that they were fit and from the description, the shot must have covered over 100 yards. The ground measures 25 acres and, like on the maidans of Mumbai, many matches are held simultaneously. No wonder the ball kept on travelling!

In 1900, a brief experiment was carried out at Lord's for just a few matches. Netting three-feet high ringed the boundary and if the ball hit the netting across the turf, the batsmen would get two runs added to whatever had been run. If it cleared the netting, they would get three additional runs. This was introduced because, apparently, it was felt that too many runs had been scored in the previous season. However, the new system was considered unfair to big hitters and soon scrapped. It did however result in a freak incident where Samuel Hill Wood for Derbyshire versus MCC, in his second innings of 43, made a stroke off the bowling of C.J. Burnup which resulted in 10 runs including overthrows.

In an August 1932 county championship match for Nottinghamshire, in their first innings versus Northamptonshire at Kettering, Arthur Staples struck a ball from E.W. 'Nobby' Clarke to the offside, where it fell inches short of crossing the boundary. By the time fielder Vallance Jupp threw it in, Staples and his partner Willis Walker were crossing for the fifth run. The throw at the bowler's end missed the stumps and went for four overthrows, thus ensuring that Staples gained nine runs from one ball.

The incident was recalled by the Northamptonshire captain W.C. Brown in a letter to the editor in the February 1966 issue of *The Cricketer*, following Staples' obituary, which appeared in the October 1965 issue and briefly mentioned the incident.

The final of the inaugural 1975 World Cup, between Australia and West Indies at Lord's, witnessed two unusual incidents. West Indies' dynamic opening batsman Roy Fredericks hooked Dennis Lillee and even as all eyes were on the ball crossing the boundary, the batsman's foot nudged the bail and he was out hit wicket.

Then, the Australian last wicket pair of Lillee and Jeff Thomson came together at 233 in reply to West Indies' 291 for eight. Amidst mounting tension as the runs ticked away, Thomson was 'caught' by Fredericks in the deep and thousands of fans invaded the field, thinking that it was all over. But they had not noticed umpire Tom Spencer signal a no-ball. Amidst the mayhem, the batsmen kept running, even as the police cleared the field so that the match could resume.

When umpire Dickie Bird asked Lillee how many he had run, he replied, 'You should be keeping count. But I make it about 17.'

Bird wrote in his autobiography:

I had to disappoint Lillee by telling him I was giving him only 4 out of the 17 for his gallant running exploits. Fredericks, after catching the ball, had hurled it at the stumps in a bid to pull off another run-out off a no-ball. It missed and disappeared into the middle of the onrushing tidal wave of spectators. According to the laws, we had, therefore, to award 4 runs and call 'dead ball' due to 'interference with the ball'—much to Lillee's breathless disgust.

In Test matches, there have been five instances of eight runs from one ball due to overthrows, including on one occasion in Bombay in 1951–52. Vijay Hazare, in his innings of 155, drove Brian Statham and Hazare, and Pankaj Roy ran four. Statham collected Frank Ridgway's throw from the outfield but in his attempt to run-out Roy, Statham's throw missed the stumps and the ball crossed the boundary.

Overthrows, which resulted in six runs being awarded due to an umpire's blunder, also played a crucial role in England winning the 2019 ICC World Cup final against New Zealand at Lord's (see Chapter 1).

In fact, 36 runs is not the maximum possible off one over if the bowler keeps bowling no-balls. Then, theoretically, the sky is the limit and the record for most runs off one over is a staggering 77 runs from an over lasting 22 balls, including 16 deliberate no-balls. That particular incident brought the game into disrepute and is not considered a legitimate record.

It happened during a domestic match in Christchurch, New Zealand between Canterbury and Wellington in February 1990. Wellington captain Ervin McSweeney declared, setting Canterbury 291—a win for either side would take them to the top of the points table. With the score reading 108 for 8 with a possible two overs left, the captain told bowler Robert Vance to stand at the wicket and lob up inviting balls, many deliberate no-balls (17 in all, 15 in succession!) in an effort to get the batsmen to make rash strokes and lose their wickets.

Lee Germon smashed 70 runs off that ludicrous over but such was the confusion that the players, umpires and scorers all lost track of the events. Canterbury fell just one run short, with Richard Petrie in all the confusion defending the final ball of the match. The result was not clear till late in the evening and such a farce has thankfully never been attempted again.

The record for most runs in a List A over also occurred in New Zealand on 7 November 2018 at Hamilton in the Ford Trophy and the luckless bowler was Central Districts' South Africa-born medium pace bowler Willem Ludick. The two Northern Districts batsmen Joe Carter and Brett Hampton combined to strike six sixes, and with two no-balls added to the over (both for height), the sequence read 4, 6 (no-ball), 6 (no-ball), 6, 1, 6, 6 and 6. The total of 43 runs beat the previous record of 39 set in 2013 in Bangladesh.

Then, in an IPL match at Sharjah on 22 September 2020, a massive 27 runs were scored off just two legitimate deliveries, with Rajasthan Royal's Englishman Joffra Archer at the crease. The unfortunate bowler was Chennai Super King's South African Lungi Ngidi in the final over of Rajasthan's innings. The first two legitimate balls were hit for 6; then came two no-balls (one run penalty for each) which meant free-hits and these also went for 6 each. And the next was a wide, so one more run was added to the total—27 from two and 30 runs in all from that over!

Such is cricket's fascination for the sixer that two books have been written specifically on the subject. Gerald Brodribb's *Hit for Six* was released in 1960. Indian-born Sydney-based author Kersi Meher-Homji's *Six Appeal: On Soaring Sixes and Lusty Six-Hitters* came out in 1996.

Indian Icons

It was an Indian cricketer who, in 1926, hit the headlines with the world record for most sixes in a first-class innings.

That innings by C.K. Nayudu not only sent the 25,000 spectators at the Bombay Gymkhana into a tizzy, it also helped kick-start the creation of the BCCI two years later and in 1932, India's entry into the elite club of Test-playing nations.

On the first day of the two-day match (30 November–1 December) between MCC and the Hindus, it was Guy Earle who enthralled the crowd with his six-hitting feat. His innings of 130 contained eight sixes and 11 fours.

However, that was only the precursor to the spectacle that unfolded the next day. There were 11 sixes and 13 fours in Nayudu's 153, his century arriving in just 65 minutes. Those soaring sixes eclipsed the previous best of 10 in a first-class innings. The current record stands at 23 by Colin Munro of New Zealand, the same as the List A mark held by Australia's D'Arcy Short.

MCC captain Arthur Gilligan had this to stay about Nayudu's batting: 'A really great batsman—I cannot find enough words to express my opinion of him. His polished display of batsmanship such as he gave was one of the best I have ever seen.'

According to journalist Berry Sarbadhikary, 'His strokes terrified the fieldsmen, dazzled everybody's eyesight, broke all rules of batting, science and logic, and stirred the crowd to wonder and delight.'

Nayudu's six-hitting feat made him the centre of attraction on the maiden 1932 tour of England and spectators flocked to see him in action. In the match against Warwickshire at Edgbaston, he hooked a ball which cleared the River Rea, and as the river then formed the boundary between Warwickshire and Worcestershire, this was a rare example of 'hitting the ball into the next county'. It was one of six sixes in an innings of 162.

Fittingly, it was Nayudu himself who led India in their very first Test at Lord's.

Fast forward to Lord's 1990, and replying to England's mammoth 653 for 4 declared, India lost their ninth wicket at 430, with 24 needed to clear the follow-on. Kapil Dev was joined by last man and rank bunny Narendra Hirwani. The champion all-rounder, on his fourth and final Test tour of England, did what came naturally—after blocking the first two balls of the over, he smashed hapless off spinner Eddie Hemmings for four consecutive sixes, the first time this feat had been achieved in a Test match.

Follow-on averted, Hirwani was out to the very next ball bowled by Angus Fraser. Though India eventually lost by 247 runs and despite the match featuring a world-record batting feat by England captain Graham Gooch and a sensational century by his counterpart Mohammad Azharuddin, it is Kapil's audacious feat that is remembered most to this day.

In his autobiography *Straight From the Heart*, Kapil explained his thought process.

If I were to go into the technique, I remember how I employ the most uncomplicated means while toying with Hemmings...The lesson is, if you want to hit over the top, make sure you've the skill to do it successfully. I've always had this free-spirited approach to the game of cricket. This is how I lofted four successive sixes. That's the way I've always played—competitively and aggressively.

In the book *Cricket's Greatest Battles: Classic Matches Analysed by England's Most Astute Captains,* Nasser Hussain claimed that the battle had been more like Kapil Dev versus Gooch rather than versus Hemmings:

> All credit to Kapil Dev for calling Gooch's bluff; the Indian all-rounder pressed G for gamble and it came off. Knowing that Kapil liked to hit in the air, Gooch laid down the challenge: 'The only way you're going to get past the follow-on is to hit Eddie for four sixes. We'll put two men back, and have a go if you want to.' He did have a go. Four times. And hit them all for six.

It was in the 1983 Prudential World Cup, memorably won by the team that he led, that Kapil Dev had unleashed a flurry of sixes when India were staring down the barrel of defeat and elimination at the hands of debutants Zimbabwe at Tunbridge Wells. That eye-popping innings of 175 not out contained six sixes and 16 fours (see Chapter 7).

Shastri Emulates Sobers

If a poll had been conducted among cricket fans in the 1980s as to the batsman least likely to emulate Sobers and his six sixes, Ravi Shastri (and Pakistan's Mudassar Nazar) would have been near the top. Shastri's strokeplay was largely limited to pushes, nudges and glances—the last his bread-and-butter shot, which Sunil Gavaskar described as the 'chapati shot' for the way Shastri rolled his wrists in executing it.

Having made his debut in New Zealand in 1981 on the strength of his left-arm spin, Shastri had since developed his batting to such an extent that he was one of India's leading batsman in the home series against England in 1984–85 which the visitors won 2-1. And just two months later, he would be crowned 'Champion of Champions' in the World Championship of Cricket in Melbourne (see Chapter 10).

Shastri scored centuries in the first Test at Bombay and the third at Calcutta, which ended just a couple of days before the start of the Ranji Trophy match versus Baroda. That Calcutta century was painfully slow, taking nearly eight hours and contributed to a dire drawn game.

In fact, Shastri was lucky to be in the playing XI at all in Bombay. Both he and pace bowler Raju Kulkarni had been dropped by captain Gavaskar in the previous Ranji Trophy tie against Gujarat for arriving at the ground after the 9 a.m. toss. Shastri was to give Kulkarni a lift but got delayed. As a result, Shastri was reduced to 12th man duties and Kulkarni was banished to the press box as scorer!

The three-day West Zone league match was meandering to a draw on the final day (10 January 1985), with Gavaskar content to sit on the first innings lead. But Shastri's blitz post-tea gave him the luxury of a declaration.

That blitz saw Shastri set the record for the fastest double century in first-class cricket (113 minutes; 123 balls), all due to one over from occasional left-arm spinner Tilak Raj.

'I was a confused bowler,' said the hapless Raj after the match, duplicating Nash's 'record' of being hit for six sixes in an over. 'I was aware of Sobers' record. I tried my best to contain him. But it was his day.' Shaken and shell-shocked— unlike Nash—he refused to pose for photos with Shastri, whose 13 sixes overtook the previous Indian record of 11 by Nayudu, made 59 years earlier in the same city.

It was only the late photographer Thomas Rocha who captured all the sixes while on duty for the *The Hindu* daily and their sister publication, *Sportstar* weekly.

Shastri was making his writing debut for the Calcutta-based

Sportsworld weekly and marked it with a description of his feat in the 30 January–5 February 1985 issue.

> It was after the fourth six that I became aware of the record and how near I was to it. I decided to go for it. The fifth delivery was fastish, pitching around middle and leg. I lifted the ball into the stands at mid on. I knew now that I had to go all out; it was now or never. I was aware that Tilak Raj would try his hardest to contain me. No bowler likes to be hit for one six, let alone six in an over. I took a step outside the leg stump. Tilak Raj pitched it outside the off. Again—possibly because of my reach—I was able to lunge towards the ball and hit it straight. The ball landed with a thud on the sightscreen. I had done it! The crowd went cuckoo with delight while I was dizzy, on top of the world and elated. I have always been an ardent admirer of Sobers. Viswanath and he have been my two heroes.

'They'll think it is the eighth wonder of the world,' was what Shastri said when asked how he thought Calcutta cricket fans would react to his batting blitz, so soon after his crawl in the Eden Gardens Test!

Just as one English spectator (Richard Stokes) had been present at Old Trafford and New Delhi for Jim Laker's all-10 in 1956 and Anil Kumble's repeat feat in 1999, and only the late Bob Woolmer (as an 11-year-old) had been witness to both Hanif Mohammad's 499 in 1959 and Brian Lara's 501 not out in 1994 (as the Warwickshire coach), so one journalist was present both at Swansea and Bombay to witness the stupendous shot-making of Sobers and Shastri. That was the late Dicky Rutnagur, the Indian-born and England-based journalist who was in India to report on the ongoing India-England series.

Nash was both surprised and relieved that it had happened again. 'Surprised because it took the best part of 100 years to happen the first time [in 1968]; now it has happened again within 17 years. I'm relieved too that I am no longer the only bowler who has suffered such an indignity, although it has never bothered me that much.'

Both were bowling slow left-arm spin when they got the treatment. Nash, though, finished his career with 993 first-class wickets while Raj had just five.

If Shastri emulating Sobers was a shock, Yuvraj repeating the feat was far less so. He was, after all, one of the cleanest strikers of the ball in world cricket.

World Cup Wonders

No batsman had struck six sixes in an over in international cricket in 130 years—and then it happened twice within six months in 2007.

First it was Gibbs in the ICC World Cup (50 overs) in West Indies, followed by Yuvraj Singh in the inaugural ICC T20 World Cup in South Africa.

In his very first innings in international cricket, in Nairobi in 2000 as a teenager, Yuvraj had smashed the mighty Australian bowling attack for 84 runs at better than a-run-a-ball. Now India was facing England at Kingsmead, Durban on 19 September in a virtual knockout, with the winner assured of a place in the semifinals.

Yuvraj had struck two boundaries off Andrew Flintoff's 18th over. Reportedly, the English all-rounder uttered threatening words to Yuvraj and this fired him up.

India were at 173 for three, with captain Dhoni at the non-striker's end. Fast bowler Stuart Broad faced Yuvraj's wrath that evening, as he raced to the quickest half-century (12 balls) in any form of international cricket, though matched by Gayle and Zazai in T20 domestic.

The match was won by India, so were the semifinal and final. Following the disaster in the 50-overs World Cup, where India had been knocked out in the first round, the victory in South Africa brought new life into Indian cricket. It also led to the formation of the Indian Premier League the next year and cricket would never be the same again—for better or for worse!

Sealed with a Six

The only World Cup final to be won with a six? That was in 2011, on 2 April to be precise, at the Wankhede Stadium and it was captain Dhoni who smote Nuwan Kulasekara high and handsome in the penultimate over of the match. India were world champs again after a long gap of 28 years.

Dhoni had made the calculated move of promoting himself over the in-form Yuvraj, with India in a nervy position at the fall of the third wicket. He has struck 370 sixes in his international career and 209 in 190 IPL matches till the end of 2019, but none has been more vital than this one, which went soaring into the Mumbai night sky.

On 18 March 2018, the final of the Nidahas T20 Trophy was being played at the R. Premadasa Stadium, Colombo. Bangladesh had India at their mercy at 133 for 5: the equation read 34 runs to win in 12 balls.

Enter Dinesh Karthik to play a stunning cameo. The wicketkeeper smashed 22 runs in the penultimate over, but 12 more were needed in the final bowled by Soumya Sarkar. The last ball of the match, five to win and Karthik strikes it for 6. This remains the only occasion till the end of 2019 (1,024 matches) that a T20I match has ended with a six when five runs were needed off the last ball to win. It's rare that a score of 29 can be considered match-winning, but then this came from eight balls at the end of the innings.

Rohit Sharma had earned the tag of 'Nohit' Sharma on social media for his relatively poor record in Tests, though he is a leading batsman in white ball matches. All that changed when South Africa toured India for three Tests in late 2019. The visitors were whitewashed but the breakthrough came with Rohit's promotion to opener. The 19 sixes hit by him were the most by any batsman in a Test series and that too in just three Tests. The Indian team total of 47 was also a series world record as was the total of 65 by both sides combined.

But at the end of the day, the fact remains—whatever our expert commentators may be told to say by the sponsors—a six is not a 'maximum'!

4

THE MANY MYTHS OF 'MANKADING'

Just call it a run-out.

—Simon Taufel

Few actions cause as much debate—at times fiery and even irrational—among cricketers, journalists and fans as the form of dismissal which has come to be known colloquially as 'Mankading'.

India's immortal all-rounder Mulvantrai Himmatlal Mankad, known to one and all as Vinoo, entered the cricket history books as the first bowler in a Test match to run-out the non-striker while in the act of delivering the ball.

In plain and simple terms, this mode of dismissal is nothing but a run-out. But at international level (Tests, ODIs and T20Is) it is still a rare sight. Many who use the term 'Mankading' appear blissfully unaware of Mankad's remarkable feats. It could be said that his name lives on thanks to the term. But the fact is that it has a stigma attached to it—which itself is ludicrous—and does not do justice to his name and memory.

It is for this reason that the Mankad family, which includes his late Test cricketer son Ashok and two others who played first-class cricket, the late Atul and the youngest Rahul, who is in his sixties, have sought over the years to have the term, unofficial though it is, erased from cricket's lexicon, much as the term 'Chinaman', used to describe a type of spinner's delivery, but which has racist overtones and has been removed by numerous publications.

So what term can be used in its place? Ace umpire Simon Taufel of Australia, when I met him in New Delhi in November 2019, was infuriated by the furore this form of dismissal always causes and exclaimed, 'Just call it a run out!'

To differentiate from a conventional run out, I have always used the term 'so-called Mankading', but perhaps the best term would be 'bowler's run out', BRO in short.

This focus on the one incident in Mankad's illustrious career also tends to obscure the fact that he remains the only all-rounder in Test cricket history to score two double centuries (that too in the same series) and take eight wickets in an innings on two occasions with his brilliant left-arm spin. He reached the double of 1,000 runs and 100 wickets in his 23rd Test in November 1952, a world record that stood for 27 years before England's Ian Botham did it in his 21st Test. And the 1952 Lord's Test has been immortalized as 'Mankad's Match' for his lion-hearted all-round display.

Twice on India's inaugural tour of Australia in 1947–48, Mankad pulled off a rare act, with opener Bill Brown falling victim on both occasions. The second occasion was the first time it had been seen in a Test match and so it caused quite a stir.

The first occasion was when India defeated An Australian XI (as the team was called) at Sydney in November 1947, their best performance on that tour, in which they lost four of the five Tests by large margins, the one draw at Sydney being rain-affected.

Mankad took eight wickets in the second innings—and had a hand in one more (the run out)—as the home side collapsed for 203, to lose by 47 runs. The eight included the wicket of the peerless Don Bradman. But it was Bradman's century in the first innings, his 100th first-class hundred, that grabbed all the headlines.

Brown's run-out in the second innings for 30 was described thus in *The Cricketer* (Spring Annual 1948): 'Brown was run out, backing up, by the bowler, Mankad, after he had had an earlier warning. The crowd realized the fairness of the bowler's action *and cheered him*.' (emphasis mine)

'Ginty' Lush in the *Sunday Telegraph* (14 December 1947) wrote that Mankad 'had Brown at his mercy, he beckoned the batsman back with a crooked finger when Brown was a yard out of his ground [before eventually running him out]. This was hailed as one of the most sporting acts ever seen at the SCG.'

The famous Australian leg spinner of the 1920s, Arthur Mailey, felt that Mankad was 'over generous' and sporting in not running him out 'because Brown had taken an advantage.'

Mailey recounts that Brown was dropped in the next over, bowled by captain Lala Amarnath and then when Mankad came back to bowl, he broke the wicket with Brown nearly two feet outside the crease. 'Brown walked off the ground looking crestfallen. But it would have been too much to have expected three "lives" in three successive overs.' ('Brown Ignores Indian Bowler's Caution: Run Out', *Daily Telegraph*, 19 November 1947)

In the *Courier Mail* dated 19 December 1947 ('Why Mankad Traps Brown'), L.H. Kearney made some startling revelations:

> When in Brisbane recently, Vinoo told me his reason, under a promise that I would not divulge it until he had trapped Brown a second time, as he expected he would. Being a left-arm bowler, Mankad had confided in me that Brown by leaving the popping crease and advancing forward but outside the pitch, completely distracts him, as he is half face on to the moving Brown when the ball leaves his hand. 'My reflective vision becomes affected and my bowling concentration suffers,' said Mankad. 'I warned Brown in Sydney [in the earlier match] not to leave the non-striker's popping crease until the ball had left my hand, but Brown ignored the warning,' said Mankad.
>
> Mankad explained that a right arm bowler is not similarly embarrassed by the moving non-striking batsman as when the ball leaves the hand of the right-arm bowler he has no 'sight' of the batsman attempting to 'steal a march' on him. Some argue that Mankad's trap is not cricket. That is ridiculous. Why not similarly claim that it is unfair for the batsman to 'back up' hoping for a quick 'stolen' run?

However, unlike in the previous match that was also at Sydney, when Mankad repeated the dismissal of Brown on the second day (13 December) of the third Test, it did create something of a furore, as this time Mankad did not warn Brown about his transgression.

Here is Lush again ('Mankad Again Traps Bill Brown', *Sunday Telegraph*, 14 December 1947):

Brown's dismissal caused heated discussion in the members' stand. Even the Press box was the scene of a debate as to whether Mankad was guilty of a sporting breach. The history of the Brown-Mankad duel is: Brown warned by Mankad for backing up too smartly in the India v. An Australian XI match at the SCG. Brown run-out by Mankad in the same match for offending again. Brown run-out for the second time by Mankad yesterday. When Brown was trapped yesterday it was obvious that he was disgusted with himself. When the umpire gave him out, Brown raised his arm and swung it through the air in disgust. Although a run-out in this fashion is permissible, it is not regarded as a sportsmanlike thing under ordinary circumstances. But in the light of a previous warning, and a dismissal, Brown was foolish to take liberties with Mankad. And a foot gained at the bowler's end is still a foot gained at the wicketkeeper's end. However, Brown's backing-up was not as exaggerated as when he last played in Sydney. Mankad can scarcely be called a bad sport for trapping Brown. As Mankad bowls left-hand round the wicket, he has an excellent view of anyone trying to get a 'lead out' from the popping-crease. The first time [he warned Brown]. Yesterday there was no warning—just lightning-like action.

In the *Truth*, Sydney (21 December 1947), an unnamed reporter states that Mankad 'has been the victim of a little biting criticism' for the run out, which the reporter defends. The reporter then writes that he asked Mankad if he had warned the batsman in the Test as he did in the previous match. 'No, I did not,' Mankad replied. 'But Morris did!' Morris was the batsman on strike. Mankad heard Morris say: 'Look out, Bill, you are doing the same thing again.'

In *The News*, Adelaide (15 December 1947), under the headline 'Mankad's Action Strongly Upheld', Lawrie Jervis spoke to a wide range of Australian cricket personalities who all supported Mankad. Jervis also narrates an incident on 8 November, barely a week before the first Mankad/Brown dismissal.

Bowler Martin Chappell in an Adelaide 'A' Grade match for Prospect at Prospect, South Australia, ran out non-striker Neil Kennett of Kensington when he backed up: Chappell 'halted in his run and took off the bails with Kennett six inches out of his ground.'

Martin, incidentally, is the father of the Chappell brothers, Ian, Greg and Trevor—and middle son Greg emulated his father when he became the first in an ODI to run a batsman out in this manner, at Melbourne versus England on 1 January 1975, the batsman being Brian Luckhurst. Like father like son, indeed!

There was a fallout of the Mankad/Brown Test dismissal as narrated by R.S. Whitington.[5] The Sydney crowd, while applauding Mankad's sportsmanship in the previous match, reacted unfavourably when it happened again in the Test match without a warning to Brown this time.

Under the amusing heading 'Relations between Brown and Vinoo Mankad are perfect—Mankad Wouldn't Run Him Out for all the Tea in India, let alone China', Whitington wrote that when Brown heard Mankad was hurt over the incident, he called him and 'told Mankad not to worry any more—that he, Brown, was to blame. Mankad admitted, however, that he was still upset. Brown suggested a drink. Mankad, a strict teetotaller, said he was sorry, he could not accept. However,

---

[5]*Sun*, Sydney, 21 January 1948

M.S. Ranvirsinhji [a playing member of the touring party], nephew of the famous Ranji, will deputise for him.'

Sudhir Vaidya in his 1969 biography of the cricketer (*Vinoo Mankad*) wrote: 'This [the Sydney Test run out] led to a terrific commotion in Australia and quite a few questioned his sportsmanship while many fully appreciated his action. However, Mankad's action was quite legitimate...'

To the eternal credit of Brown (who passed away in 2008 aged 96; he played in 22 Tests), he had always taken full responsibility for his actions and never pinned any of the blame on Mankad.

Many years after the incident, Brown told Rahul Mankad, 'Vinoo had done nothing against the rules. By backing up despite his warnings, I deserved it.'[6]

Indeed, Mankad was well within his rights under the MCC Laws. At that time, the 1947 Laws covering this type of dismissal were not in the run-out section, but under No Ball (Law 27) and came under the Notes section.

In 2017, the Law was further amended to make it clear that the non-striker was entirely at fault if he left his crease early (details later in this chapter).

The famous Australian opening batsman-turned-journalist Jack Fingleton had this to say in his report for *Indian Cricket* annual 1948–49:

> Mankad was a magnificent fieldsman to his own bowling and covered wide stretches of ground on both sides of the pitch. Two wickets are not shown to him in statistics of the tour. Twice he ran out Brown for leaving the crease before the ball was bowled and no odium attached to

[6]Anindya Dutta, *Wizards: The Story of Indian Spin Bowling*, Westland Publications, 2019

Mankad because he had given Brown frequent warnings that the latter was taking advantage.

There have been calls over the years by, among others, Sunil Gavaskar, Mumbai-based sports journalist Clayton Murzello and editor Kunal Pradhan ('Cricket a Gentleman's Game? Pshaw!', *Hindustan Times*, 30 March 2019) to rename it 'Browning' or 'Browned' considering that Brown was the culprit, not Mankad.

Before the initial Mankad/Brown run out, it had occurred a total of 15 times, including twice in India. The first instance of this dismissal in first-class cricket goes as far back as 1835. Thomas Barker (Sussex) was the bowler and George Baigent of Nottinghamshire the non-striker at New Forest Ground, Notts. Barker must have been something of a maverick, as the next four occasions of this type of dismissal were all at his hands.

The Yorkshire Herald in its scorecard gave the dismissal as 'stumped Barker', such was the sense of surprise at this innovation back then.

The Nottingham Review and General Advertiser for the Midland Counties reported it thus (11 September 1835): 'Baigent who had been in the habit of leaving his ground before the ball was delivered, was put out very cleverly by Barker.'

The first and only previous occasion to the Brown/Mankad dismissals in a first-class match in Australia was in January 1862 by Ray Kinloch, with John Huddleston the batsman at the receiving end, for New South Wales versus Victoria at Melbourne.

In a report in *The Age*, Melbourne, dated 10 January 1862, the run-out is described as 'an old schoolboy trick'. Notably, it states: 'A round of applause greeted this successful bit of legerdemain.'

The last word should go to none other than the Australian captain Don Bradman:

> For the life of me I cannot understand why...in some quarters Mankad's sportsmanship was questioned. The laws of cricket make it quite clear that the non-striker must keep within his ground until the ball has been delivered. If not, why is the provision there which enables the bowler to run him out?
>
> By backing up too far regularly the non-striker is very obviously gaining an unfair advantage. On numerous occasions he may avoid being run-out at the opposite end by gaining this false start...Mankad was so scrupulously fair that he first of all warned Brown before taking any action. There was absolutely no feeling in the matter as far as we were concerned, for we considered it quite a legitimate part of the game.

Bradman made two errors in this passage though. Firstly, he mis-states that the first run-out happened in the Indians' match versus Queensland. Secondly, he claims that only a spinner could pull off such a run-out off their own bowling. 'Imagine, for instance, Ray Lindwall stopping himself right at the bowling crease. He could not do it. Only the slower types of bowlers have a chance.'

In fact, there have been nine instances in international cricket—four each in Tests and ODIs and one in T20I—and five of these have been by pace bowlers, including the express Charlie Griffith of West Indies.

The most famous let-off was in the 1987 Reliance World Cup match between West Indies and Pakistan in Lahore. But more on that later.

India's stand-in captain Virender Sehwag withdrew his appeal under pressure from umpires Paul Reiffel (a former Australian fast bowler) and Billy Bowden, when bowler Ravichandran Ashwin caught non-striker Lahiru Thirimanne of Sri Lanka outside his crease in the Commonwealth Bank ODI tri-series in Brisbane on 21 February 2012.

Why the umpires should have done so is a mystery, as Ashwin was well within the rules, or 'Laws' as they are known in cricket. After the match, Sehwag would claim that Ashwin had warned the batsman first, but this was disputed by Lanka's captain Mahela Jayawardene, who said that there should have been an 'official' warning—when such an action does not exist under the Laws. He also invoked the 'spirit of the game', which is always brought up by the side on the receiving end, no matter how many times they have blotted their own copybooks by on-field actions. In fact, after the reprieve, Thirimanne was seen repeatedly stealing an unfair advantage at the non-striker's end, thus making a mockery of the Law, not to mention the 'spirit'.

Sure enough, the shoe was on the other foot in the fifth and final ODI between Sri Lanka and England at Edgbaston on 3 June 2014. Jayawardene was not the captain in this match, but he was on the field when teammate Sachitra Senanayake caught non-striker Joss Buttler out of his crease and removed the bails—BRO!

This time, there were no protestations of 'spirit of the game' from the Lankan camp!

Ashwin was in the thick of things again in the IPL, as captain of Kings XI Punjab in the match against Rajasthan Royals at Jaipur on 25 March 2019, and it was Buttler once again at the receiving end. With the IPL being such a high-profile event, it attracted attention from around the cricket world.

The BRO was pulled off on the fifth ball of the 13th over and when the decision was sent to the TV umpire Bruce Oxenford, he ruled it out. It was spotted that Buttler had been wandering out of his crease for the two deliveries when he was at the non-striker's end in the same over, and the eagle-eyed Ashwin grabbed his chance when he got it. As captain of KXIP, there was no way he was going to withdraw his appeal and the on-field umpires did not pressure him to do so, as in the ODI seven years earlier.

Like Banquo's ghost in William Shakespeare's *Macbeth*, the 'spirit of cricket' was once again invoked to haunt the game. Former players from England and Australia were particularly vocal in their condemnation of Ashwin. Among them were Shane Warne, Kevin Pietersen, Michael Vaughan and Paul Collingwood.

Very few cricketers past or present have not, at some time or the other, bent the rules/Laws and, indeed, the 'spirit', to suit themselves and their team; the exploits of Warne, Pietersen and Vaughan in this regard are too well known to cricket followers to elaborate.

Most interesting to me was Collingwood who, like the others, called Ashwin's action disgraceful. I responded by posting a video from 2008 on Twitter, tagging the former England white ball captain and asking him for his reaction. There has been none to date and no wonder.

On 25 June 2008 at the Oval, Collingwood was captain when New Zealand's Grant Elliot collided with bowler Ryan Sidebottom, was sent sprawling, was injured and run out. The umpire asked Collingwood if he wished to withdraw the appeal but he declined. A livid New Zealand captain Daniel Vettori and his teammates celebrated raucously as they scrambled home by one wicket from the final ball.

Collingwood, under pressure from the authorities and in a bid to escape censure, issued a contrite apology the next day.

But if New Zealand had lost, there would surely have been repercussions.

Just as with the Lankans, cricket karma played its hand the very next year, when Collingwood was recalled by Vettori in the Champions Trophy match in Johannesburg. There was no obstruction this time, and Collingwood was clearly at fault as he wandered out of his crease on the last ball of the over before the umpire had made the call, and wicketkeeper Brendon McCullum ran him out. Vettori had no hesitation in withdrawing the appeal, perhaps as much to prove a point as anything else.

There have also been instances of BRO in the ICC Under-19 World Cup, which leads to much tut-tutting about youngsters imbibing bad habits.

So what is this 'spirit of cricket' all about? In the May 2019 issue of *The Cricketer*, former England pace bowler and columnist Mike Selvey punched holes in the whole concept in his column headlined 'Spirit of Cricket is the Game's Unicorn', while focusing on the Ashwin/Buttler incident.

Selvey did not let Ashwin off the hook as he, among others, felt it was a 'shabby premeditated action by the bowler'. He admitted to being ambivalent about this particular incident though he has always stridently defended the bowler's right to employ the BRO, pinning the blame on the non-striker for leaving his crease and refers to Buttler as a 'serial wanderer'.

Selvey writes:

> The real controversy though, was that this time Buttler was in his ground at the point he might have expected Ashwin to deliver the ball, only for the bowler to apparently abort his action—selling him a dummy in other words—so that the batsman's momentum took him out of the crease.

This was strongly refuted by left-arm spinner Murali Kartik in a conversation with me. Kartik holds some sort of an Indian record, having pulled off the BRO five times—once for his county Surrey in 2012 and twice more in first-class cricket, as well twice in List A matches for Railways. Kartik is of the opinion that the non-striker must leave the crease only once the ball is actually released.

Law 42.15, which covered this form of dismissal, was amended in 2017 to put the onus on the non-striker to remain in his ground. The tweaking of the original Law comes under 41.16 and two changes have been made under the title 'Leaving his/her ground early':

1. Extending the point at which the run-out of the non-striker can be attempted to the instant at which point the bowler would be expected to release the ball. This will have the effect of keeping the non-striker in his/her ground for longer.

2. Changing the title of the Law, to put the onus on the non-striker to remain in his/her ground. It is often the bowler who is criticized for attempting such a run out, but it is the batsman who is attempting to gain the advantage. The message to the non-striker is very clear—if you do not want to risk being run out, stay within your ground until the bowler has released the ball.

The extension for the time frame for the run-out has been in place for some time in the international game and the Law change is in line with this.

The wording of the second clause should surely have put to rest any unseemly fuss but, as subsequent events prove, this is far from the case.

The MCC, who are the custodians of the Laws of the game (not rules, mind you), first issued a statement stating that Ashwin's action was within the spirit of the game and then shortly after retracted it.

According to Fraser Stewart, the MCC's manager of the Laws of cricket was quoted in the *Daily Telegraph* (UK), saying, 'Having extensively reviewed the incident again, and after reflection we don't think it is within the spirit of the game.'

'We believe the pause was too long between the time Ashwin reached the crease and the moment it was reasonable to expect the ball would be delivered,' Stewart added. 'When Buttler could have reasonably expected the ball to be delivered, he was in his ground. We now think that at the key moment, Buttler was in his ground.'

At the same time, Buttler also came in for criticism. 'Buttler, it's fair to say, did not make a concerted effort to get back into his crease after Ashwin had delayed his delivery, and didn't help himself in that respect.' Stewart added, 'It's also unfair and against the spirit of cricket for non-strikers to leave their ground too early. All these debates wouldn't be necessary if non-strikers remained in their ground until the ball is on its way down the pitch.'

However, Simon Taufel's defence of Ashwin's action should have settled the issue once and for all. The award-winning umpire claimed that it had nothing to do with the spirit of the game and everything to do with Law 38 which covers run-outs, as he said he had explained to the MCC.

Said Taufel, 'For him [Ashwin] to be subject to adverse commentary that amounted to character assassination regarding his supposed contravention of the spirit of the game, is incredibly unfair, in the way the Laws are written and the way they are to be applied.' Taufel doubled down on this when I asked him about the controversy when we met in New Delhi.

The issue was once again front and centre when the IPL

moved to the Gulf in 2020. Ashwin and Ricky Ponting found themselves in the same team (Delhi Capitals, previously Delhi Daredevils), with the former Australian captain as coach.

Before the start of the tournament, Ponting had appeared on Ashwin's podcast, where they discussed the issue after Ponting had made it clear that he would not approve of any such action on Ashwin's part.

Indian cricket followers were quick to recall the acrimonious 2008 Sydney Test when Ponting was captain. The late English cricketer and columnist Peter Roebuck had called for Ponting's sacking in the aftermath of the storm over the Test, referring to the Australian team under his charge as 'a pack of wild dogs' in his column for the *Sydney Morning Herald.*

On 5 October in Dubai, in the match against Royal Challengers Bangalore, Ashwin paused in his delivery stride (the fifth of the third over) with ball in hand, but did not run-out Aaron Finch (incidentally an Australian) who was at least a yard out of his crease. The cameras panned to a smiling Ponting on the DC team bench. Later, Ashwin tweeted: 'Let's make it clear! First and final warning for 2020. I am making it official and don't blame me later on.' Following this, it was clarified that the player and the coach were on the 'same page'.

Gavaskar was on commentary with former New Zealand bowler Simon Doull and they both felt that the straying batsmen should pay a price. In an interview to Sriram Veera of *The Indian Express* (7 October, *'When will the Aussies learn? It was Brown in 1947, and we are in 2020'*), Gavaskar suggested, '...the TV umpire should straightaway call one run short. Even if the bowler has not tried to run (the non-striker) out and has released the ball, the third umpire should call it one-short every time.'

There is a small group of cricket followers who see the term 'Mankading' as a form of tribute. When this was put to

Gavaskar by Veera, he was quick to shoot it down. '...that is not the way the cricketing world sees it. It has a clear negative connotation.'

So what is the 'spirit of cricket' which crops up every now and then? As with archaic terms like 'it's not cricket' and 'gentleman's game', these are clichés that cricket still clings to, despite contrary historical evidence going back centuries.

In the late 90s, two former English captains, Colin Cowdrey and Ted Dexter persuaded the MCC to include the 'spirit of cricket' preamble to the Laws. Selvey wrote in his 'The Inside Track' column: 'As far as I can tell, no one has managed to clearly define what this spirit actually is. It is an abstract...Is it now time that we recognize that it's cricket's unicorn: it's a nice idea but does not really exist.'

It states: 'Cricket is a game that owes much of its appeal to the fact that it should be played not only within its Laws but also within the Spirit of the Game. Any action which is seen to abuse the Spirit causes injury to the game itself.' Suitably vague!

Predictably, Sunil Gavaskar came out with guns blazing in his 'On The Write Line' column in *Sportstar* ('Two Meaty Imbroglios!', 20 April 2019) and, like Selvey, the nebulous 'spirit of the game' was his target.

Gavaskar also took aim at an unnamed 'incompetent' Australian journalist for coining the term 'Mankading', and the Indian media for copying it.

So what about the fact that the BCCI has used the same offensive term on its website bcci.tv?

In the Vijay Hazare Trophy List A match at Jaipur on 14 October 2019, Railways' left-arm spin bowler (something he shares with Mankad and Karthik) Harsh Tyagi, seeing Bengal non-striker Agniv Pan out of the crease, removed the bails and ran him out in the 36th over of the innings.

The match ended in a tie and in a report in *The Hindu* (15 October 2019) by P.K. Ajith Kumar, headlined 'Mankading and déjà vu', Bengal coach Arun Lal (who went by the moniker Quotient King of domestic cricket during his playing days) blasted the bowler, stating, 'It is bad for cricket and the reputation of (Indian) Railways.' Even Railways coach Yusuf Ali Khan said, 'It is not good for cricket.'

Shockingly, the scorecard for the match on the BCCI website gives Pan's dismissal thus: 'Agniv Pan Mankading 28.' Two other Bengal batsmen were run-out and are listed as such, with the name of the fielder responsible. So, what was the BCCI thinking?

Other online resources such as espncricinfo.com and cricketarchive.com give the correct term for Pan's dismissal, but oddly none of the three name the fielder (in this case also the bowler) responsible, whose name is always given in the scorecard and is listed thus for the other two Bengal run-out batsmen. A query uploaded by me to BCCI on Twitter has yet to elicit a response.

Ian Chappell also weighed in favour of Ashwin and said that, as a non-striker, he never left the crease till he saw the ball leave the bowler's hand. He rubbished the idea that the batsman should be given a warning first and also decried Mankad's name being associated with what has become a controversial decision.

Henry Blofeld in his book *My A-Z of Cricket*, contends that it should be enshrined in the Law for the bowler to give a warning officially to the umpire, who would then inform the scorer. Chappell asks why a bowler should warn a non-striker, who is cheating by trying to gain some extra ground.

Further, if a batsman receives such a warning, why not a bowler for bowling his first no-ball, whereby he also cuts the crease? Or the wicketkeeper to the batsman before affecting a stumping? Whether the non-striker is doing so intentionally or just being absent-minded, the onus surely lies solely with him, to stay within the crease till the ball leaves the bowler's hand.

Selvey weighed in again in the March 2020 issue of *The Cricketer* in his 'The Inside Track' column ('Mankading is fair game'), this time after a BRO dismissal in the Under-19 World Cup in South Africa earlier that year, which once again ignited fierce debate.

> Don't you love it when the cricket world goes into meltdown over an incident that to many offends not so much the Laws of the game but the indefinable chimera known as the 'spirit of cricket'?...How difficult is it for a batsman to remain in ground until the ball is released? Honestly? There is no requirement to offer the bowler the equivalent of a mulligan when they transgress with a front-foot no-ball...This familiarly is known as 'Mankading', unfairly, particularly in the view of the family of the late Vinoo Mankad...Poor old Vinoo, acting within the Laws of the game, has been forever linked to some sort of notoriety... rather than a career as one of India's greatest cricketers.

In his earlier column in May 2019, Selvey wrote: 'There has always existed this noble idea that cricket is a "gentleman's game", but that in itself is an ambiguity, given the rascals and rapscallions that have existed in that level of society.'

Cheating, match fixing, drunken brawls, riots, all these and more have been part and parcel of cricket's history going back centuries.

The late Sir Derek Birley in his book *The Willow Wand: Some Cricket Myths Explored* (one of the inspirations of this book, see Introduction) took apart all this talk of the 'spirit of cricket', gentleman's game, etc., as did the late American

Marxist cricket writer Mike Marqusee in his book *Anyone But England*. Birley did so again in *A Social History of English Cricket*. None of these went down well with the stuffy English cricket establishment.

In the opening chapter of *The Willow Wand*, titled 'The Mythology of Cricket', Birley sets out his tone for the rest of the book by writing: 'Indeed, as we shall see, as long as there have been laws of cricket, there have been law-breakers.'

Former England captain Mike Brearley has also devoted a chapter to this issue of the so-called Mankading in his thought-provoking book *The Spirit of Cricket: Reflections on Play and Life*.

Remarkably, that bastion of English cricket establishment and MCC president in the nineteenth century, Lord Harris (then George Robert Canning Harris) was behind one such act and there was no outrage expressed over it. Playing for Eton School in their traditional match against arch-rivals Harrow at Lord's in 1870, the victim in this case was Conrad Wallroth.

Spencer Gore, the first man to win the Wimbledon tennis title in 1877, reported it thus in a book on the history of Harrow: 'Harris ... noticed that Wallroth, who was well set, was backing up too eagerly. He put himself on to bowl (quite rightly, to my mind), and, pretending to bowl, caught Wallroth tripping, and he paid the penalty.'

Cricket has always been seen as a batsman's game from the time in England when the batsmen were generally amateurs who were often titled and earned a healthy living outside the game and were invariably appointed as captain. The bowlers were the toiling professionals that came from modest financial and educational backgrounds including, most famously, the coal mines across the land.

Particularly since the advent of the IPL in 2008, and the countless T20 leagues that have mushroomed across the world, the balance of power has shifted even more dramatically towards the batsmen, much to the detriment of the game.

Hi-tech bats where edges fly over the tiny, shortened boundaries (see Chapter 3), the introduction of the 'free hit' for no-balls and other tweaks of the Laws/playing conditions, including the over-strict interpretation of wides down the leg side, have all forced the bowler to innovate and improvise in a desperate bid to regain some control, and they should be encouraged to do so rather than having their hands tied by the game's authorities.

Cricket is, after all, supposed to be a contest between bat and ball, but these days bowlers are rapidly being reduced to cannon fodder. What will be the future of cricket, if youngsters aspiring to be cricketers decide that it is just not worth their while to be bowlers?

So, what about that famous BRO let-off from that 1987 Reliance World Cup match? With the scores tied, fast bowler Courtney Walsh was about to bowl the final ball, with Abdul Qadir on strike and last man Salim Jaffer at the non-striker's end. West Indies were 216 all out, Pakistan were 215 for nine. One run would make it a tie and Pakistan would win on fewer wickets lost, as was in the tournament playing conditions.

But as Walsh ran in, he stopped in his tracks and warned Jaffer who, in his enthusiasm, was yards down the track. Jaffer scrambled back shamefacedly and Qadir then sliced the final delivery away for two runs. This effectively ended West Indies', finalists in the previous three editions of the World Cup, hopes of reaching the semifinals.

Martin Johnson, writing in *The Independent* (7 October 1987), put it in this way: 'He [Walsh] could have run-out Jaffer by half a pitch-length but opted for the warning (and a non-lynching) instead...'

Captain Vivian Richards and Walsh predictably opted for the moral high ground after the match, Richards reportedly stating, 'We don't play our cricket that way.'

As for the bowler, he said, 'That is something I could not do because that is how I was brought up...As a youngster, the spirit of the game meant a lot to me...'

Try telling that to England fast bowler and genuine tail-ender Devon Malcolm. He was the target of a fearful battering at the hands of the self-same Walsh in the 1994 Test match at Kingston, Jamaica (incidentally, Malcolm's birthplace).

Malcolm gives a vivid description of the assault in his autobiography *You Guys Are History!*, where he expressed his anguish that the umpires did not step in to put an end to the intimidation and vowed to pay back Walsh if they ever met again in a match. They did, the next year in England, but whether Malcolm followed through on his threat is not known.

Vic Marks, in his farewell piece to Walsh in the 2001 edition of *Wisden Cricketers Almanack*, was scathing:

> There were times when he [Walsh] was prepared to explore the limits of fair play. In 1994 in Jamaica, he launched a madcap assault on England's hopeless No. 11, Devon Malcolm, which could not be justified. Umpire Ian Robinson from Zimbabwe, in a shocking abnegation of his responsibilities, looked on without saying a dicky-bird. Walsh peppered Malcolm with a succession of vicious, needless bouncers. He showed no remorse for that spell.

So, here we have a situation where the bowler is breaching the Laws and posing a physical threat to a tail-ender, but is not restrained by the umpires who are empowered to do so, whereas a bowler who acts within the Law in enacting a BRO dismissal is condemned—'spirit of the game' indeed!

5

RANJI, THE LEGEND AND THE MYTH

Ranji did absolutely nothing for
Indian sport and sportsmen.

—Anthony de Mello

My introduction both to the story of Colonel His Highness Shri Sir Ranjitsinhji Vibhaji, Maharaja Jamsaheb of Nawanagar, GCSI, GBE, KCIE, aka Ranji or just 'Smith' to his teammates, and also the writing of Sir Neville Cardus, came from an English literature school textbook in 1972, when I was 13 years old.

It was the centenary of Ranji's birth and the whole country was agog with Ranji fever. A chapter on the great Indian-born English cricketer was included in our syllabus at St Xavier's School, Durgapur (West Bengal), condensed from the work of Neville Cardus, considered to be the doyen of cricket writers.

The previous year, Indian cricket had finally come of age, winning Test series in both West Indies and England, an unprecedented feat which caught the imagination of millions of youngsters, including this writer. My first taste of Cardus attracted me to cricket's rich literature. One sentence from that essay stood out, and it was only many years later that I learned that it was almost certainly a figment of Cardus' vivid imagination, a trait of his that has come in for much scrutiny in recent years.

'Bloody magic—and 'e never played a Christian stroke in his life', Cardus quoted Ted Wainwright of England and Yorkshire as saying, after Ranji had scored a century in each innings—on the same day (the first and still only occasion in first-class cricket history)—against Yorkshire at Hove in 1896, the same year as his sensational Test debut against Australia at Old Trafford.

Building on that 'quote' in an essay in *Playfair Cricket Monthly* (December 1972) to mark Ranji's birth centenary, Cardus continues:

Wainwright in saying this was being wiser than he knew:

...for the point of Ranji's genius was that he brought into English cricket an Oriental subtlety, necromancy, a perfectly un-English presence and dusky unpredictable art. We must remember...that when Ranji came to play with us, cricket was not only absolutely English; it was Victorian in its contours and spirit...No 'googlies', no jazz. If a bowler pitched down the leg side, he apologized to his captain...Ranji's famous leg glance was performed against the fastest ball, from balls on the wicket. His left leg moved gently, almost at leisure, across his right, behold!—the ball was flashing to the leg-boundary with the speed of light; and the bowler was lifting up his hands to high heaven.

Thus was born the leg glance, a stroke never seen before at least in English cricket and with it came the 'invention' of the late cut too. These wristy strokes have been carried down the centuries by Indian batsmen of the genius of G.R. Viswanath, Mohammad Azharuddin, V.V.S. Laxman and others, and have become accepted as a hallmark of Indian batsmanship.

That Ranji was a pioneer there can be no doubt, that he stood tall in the pantheon of what is considered cricket's Golden Age (the period spanning from 1890 to 1914), amongst legends like W.G. Grace, Gilbert Jessop, C.B. Fry, Sydney Barnes and Victor Trumper, is also a truism.

That his private life was remarkably opaque and that so many myths, many of them self-perpetuated, still linger over him like a halo, has become increasingly obvious over the years. But back in 1972, the glow over his centenary tended to obscure all his faults, of which there were many—though certainly not as a cricketer.

India's embracing of the legend and the man, even though he played his major cricket in England and had a hardened disdain for all things connected to Indian cricket, is not unique. The majority of our Nobel Prize winners in many fields had few connections with India save for their place of birth and, just like Ranji, made a name for themselves only after they moved to the West. Yet, Indians felt a surge of great national pride and patriotism when their awards were announced.

It was this basking in reflected glory that saw books on Ranji being released in 1972 and even India Post issuing a stamp in his honour. The Board of Control for Cricket in India also marked the occasion with a 'Ranji Centenary match' between the 'Ranji XI' led by 'Tiger' Pataudi and the Board President's XI led by S. Venkataraghavan at Jamnagar in September 1972, in which two of Australia's Ashes heroes, Bob Massie and Ross Edwards, flew down from England at the end of the Test series to participate. A glorified festival match, really given first-class status, in which Sunil Gavaskar for the President's XI recorded his best bowling figures of 3 for 43!

Goodwill messages poured in from the office of the president, the vice president, prime minister and the BCCI president, all embracing Ranji as one of our own.

Indian Cricket annual, the sister publication of Madras' famous daily *The Hindu*, published not one but two photos in their 1972 edition, captioned 'Unequalled Magic' and 'King of a Great Game' and a tribute ('Cricket's Monarch') by N.S. Ramaswami, perhaps the closest Indian equivalent in style to Cardus. Ramaswami wrote glowingly of Ranji's batsmanship, and rightly so, but he highly exaggerated and romanticized—even by official BCCI renderings—the prince's role in helping the growth of cricket in India.

In both the BCCI's *Golden Jubilee Commemoration Volume 1928-79* and the platinum jubilee publication marking 75 years of Indian Test cricket in 2008, the 'official' version on Ranji is blunt and harsh. Writing in the 1979 volume, BCCI honorary secretary Prof. M.V. Chandgadkar in his article 'History of the Board' echoes the quote at the top of this chapter.

> One would have hopefully looked at Prince Ranjitsinhji or for that matter his equally illustrious nephew, Prince Duleepsinhji, to have done something in the matter (to constitute a central controlling body). But that was not to be. It seems that although they made the cricketing world realize how good an Indian cricketer could be, they were more keen to play for England and never encouraged the efforts being made by others in India and England to create a national organization which alone would accord India and Indian cricketers international status and recognition.

In the lead essay 'The Origins...' in the platinum jubilee publication in 2008 (grandly titled *From Learners to Leaders*), Devendra Prabhudesai writes how the BCCI was desperately keen for Duleep to lead India on the 1932 inaugural tour of England, which featured the one-off Test match at Lord's.

> Not only was Duleep a prince, he was also a successful cricketer in his own right. But Duleep declined. It was later alleged that he had been asked to refuse by none other than his own uncle, who had given the impression of not being too interested in Indian cricket.

This is what apparently rankled Anthony de Mello the most. One of the pioneers of Indian sport, he was one of the founding members of the BCCI in Delhi in 1928, its first secretary and later president, and also the brains behind the staging of the first Asian Games in the new capital in 1951. Famed Indian sports journalist 'Berry' Sarbadhikary, while describing de Mello as the 'Great Dictator', also acknowledged him as 'the chief architect of modern Indian cricket'.[7]

In his seminal work *Portrait of Indian Sport*, released in 1959, de Mello pulled no punches.

> Yet and I tell it with great regret, Ranjitsinhji was never at any stage prepared to combine his roles of sportsman and Indian Prince...Ranji, in fact, did absolutely nothing for Indian sport and sportsmen.
>
> This perhaps is the greatest enigma in our sporting story. It was natural, that, when Ranji returned home [after the First World War], we should look to him for guidance on the road to cricketing recognition...It was

---

[7]Berry Sarbadhikary, *My World of Cricket: A Centenary of Tests*, Cricket Library India, 1964

right—indeed inevitable that then, and at many times in the future, those who controlled Indian cricket should turn to Ranji.

In later years, as his nephew Duleepsinhji showed signs of being a player of almost the same class, that we should again approach Ranji with the request that Duleep be encouraged to bring his cricket talents to the aid of India.

To all our requests for aid, encouragement and advice, Ranji, gave but one answer: 'Duleep and I are English cricketers.'

There is much more in what almost amounts to a rant and a slew of grievances against both Ranji and Duleep. Still, Ranji's feats undoubtedly lifted the spirits of Indians living in India and England. They had a positive effect on Indian cricket, proving to the Englishman, the custodians of the game, that it was not just a preserve of the white race.

Mukund Ramrao Jayakar, who was a law student at the height of Ranji's cricketing career and was later to become the first vice-chancellor of the University of Poona, noted in his autobiography:

Thousands of British men and women adored him, and in the worship of his skill all sense of a different nationality was drowned. When he stepped majestically out of the pavilion, what a hum of admiration went forth. As a young Indian, I used to feel so proud that one of us could evoke such admiration.

So, wittingly or unwittingly, Ranji was breaking down racial barriers. Even his trenchant, critic de Mello admitted as much.

We could be happy in the knowledge that Ranji and Duleep, by their successes on the cricket fields of England, were indirectly bringing respect and admiration to the name of Indian sport. ...I am sure that, when we came to apply to the Imperial Cricket Conference in 1929, the knowledge that our country could produce great cricketers was of the utmost assistance to us. In this indirect way, Ranji was of help...

It must be appreciated here that Ranji could be said to have discovered the prodigious talent of the legendary fast bowler/ all-rounder L. Amar Singh and his brother, the ferocious L. Ramji, who played a solitary Test match. It was on Ranji's recommendation that Amar Singh was chosen for the historic 1932 tour of England and, in partnership with Mohammad Nissar, he formed one of the finest and most fearsome opening attacks in world cricket in the 1930s. Neither of the brothers completed school and came from impoverished backgrounds. Ranji and his successors gave them employment, housing and support, and they in turn were intensely loyal to the House of Nawanagar.

Apart from the official biography of Ranji by Roland Wild in 1934, there were also biographies by Alan Ross in 1987 and then Simon Wilde's *Ranji: A Genius Rich and Strange*, in 1990, which revealed hitherto unknown murky details of the prince's life off the pitch. These involved much financial skullduggery on his part, which saw him throw lavish parties even as he approached bankruptcy, both before and after he ascended the throne of Nawanagar, which he finally did in 1907, but with loads of intrigue and suspicion involved. Lies, deceit, thievery, extortion and hints at being involved in an assassination plot, all were revealed by Wilde.

However, it was the 2003 publication of *Batting for the Empire: A Political Biography of Ranjitsinhji* by Mumbai-based journalist Mario Rodrigues that blew the lid off Ranji's intense loyalty to the British empire and his disdain not just for Indian cricket, but also for the independence movement led by fellow-Kathiawari, Mohandas Karamchand Gandhi, who was born just three years before Ranji.

The chilly reception to Rodrigues' book, mainly by ex-royalty (their privy purses and titles were abolished by Prime Minister Indira Gandhi in 1971, for which they are still resentful), was not unexpected, as Ranji has long been considered the jewel in the crown of Indian royalty. One even asked the author sarcastically if he had seen Ranji bat!

With nine pages of bibliography and four years of research, which saw him dig out files from British government archives in England (including confidential reports from the 1930s), apart from material in India, there could be no doubting Rodrigues' scholarly diligence, which led to the finding that Ranji was more loyal than the king (and queen), as the saying goes.

This was hardly unusual for the time though, as Raju Mukherji wrote in *Sportstar* ('The Other Side of Ranji'): 'Ranji, it seemed, had no inclination to see India gaining its independence. To be fair, it must be readily admitted, very few of the princely states were happy with the nationalist movement that was gaining ground in the country at the time.'

Cricket historian and Gandhi scholar Ramachandra Guha, in his foreword to Rodrigues' book, makes unflattering comparisons between Ranji and Gandhi. They were both in London at the same time. Though there is no record of their meeting, Gandhi carried a letter of introduction to his fellow-Kathiawari, as well as to three other prominent Indians, when he arrived as a student in London in 1888, one year after Ranji's own arrival. Guha writes:

But their later careers could not have been more strikingly different...One was a pillar of the British Empire; the other the Mahatma who led his people to freedom from that very Empire. What Gandhi saw as the battle for swaraj, Ranji saw as sedition. Even in their personal character they were opposed, the austerity of one contrasting with the profligacy of the other.

Famed English cricket journalist Scyld Berry devotes a chapter to Ranji in his acclaimed book *Cricket Wallah: With England in India 1981-82*, after a visit to his palace. Berry too draws an ironic comparison between the cricketer and the Mahatma: 'It is amusing to note that the beloved prince originated from a much humbler background than the Mahatma, subsequent champion of the people, who was born to the Prime Minister of Porbander.'

In fact, Ranji was not born into royalty, being an adoptive heir and that too not the first choice, so hardly a blue-blooded prince as he sought to project himself to English society through all those years of fraud, myth-making and subterfuge. He was related to the ruling Jam Sahib, but only distantly. As Berry writes:

He came from a mud-and-thatch village out in the sticks. If his contemporaries had actually seen his origins, many of them might have rejected him out of hand; if they had known he had been disinherited and was unlikely to attain the throne—that of a plague-ridden, rundown little state, as Nawanagar then was—he might have found it even harder than he did to find an opening in the game and English society. Intentionally or not [we now know it *was* intentional], Ranji deceived his contemporaries into accepting him, when otherwise they might have looked down on him as Stanley Jackson did those first two years at Cambridge. His cricket ability might never have been allowed to speak for him. But his admirers were carried away by their romanticism. 'He moved as if he had no bones', and they were inspired to think of him as a prince before he became one.

That romanticism was encouraged by Ranji who, in a conversation with the Surrey and English cricketer D.J. Knight, claimed that his batting skills were largely due to his superior eyesight which he claimed 'was just a gift of the people of my race'. This of course is nonsense, but it all added to his mystical Oriental aura and was faithfully reproduced as fact in his obituary in *The Cricketer* (6 May 1933), appearing under the initials 'F.M.': 'It is well known that both Orientals and Africans have powers of sight which are not the common birthright of the Caucasian. Thus Ranji was able to watch the ball near to its impact with the bat for a fraction of a second longer than we can.'

Pure bunkum! F.S. (Stanley) Jackson was the captain of Trinity College and Cambridge, who took a dim view of Ranji's batting in 1892, describing his style as 'dangerous cricket, with many unorthodox strokes, Ranji nearly going down on his knees to pull a ball to leg' [perhaps one of the first sweep shots seen in England], after a brief glimpse of him batting on the open field of Parker's Piece. This was an early taste of racial prejudice which he also had to also endure when he joined the Trinity College playing XI and he was ignored by his teammates.

In a twist of fate, Jackson, the future captain of England and Governor of Bengal, toured India with the second English team in 1892–93 under Lord Hawke, and this opened his eyes to the wealth of talent in Indian cricket. On his return, he gave Ranji his big break by including him in the high-profile University match against Oxford at Lord's in July 1893 and awarded him the coveted 'Blue'. Ranji had made his first-class debut a couple of months earlier. Playing for Cambridge University against the touring Australians at Fenner's the month before the Lord's Varsity match, he impressed with scores of 58 and 37 not out.

Jackson was candid enough to admit the changes wrought in his attitude after 1892–93 winter tour. 'I have no doubt my experience in India during that tour awakened in me a sympathetic interest for Indians which perhaps in 1892 I did not possess to the same degree.'

Thus, in a strange and ironic way, it was Indian cricket that gave Ranji his break, rather than the other way round, something the master batsman never publicly acknowledged. After a shaky start to his cricket career, there was no stopping Ranji as he piled on the runs for Sussex from 1895 onwards. He scored 77 not out and 150 (his maiden first-class 100) versus MCC at Lord's in his first match for the county. By 1896, he became known as the most popular man in England and the clamour now arose to have him included in the Ashes Test series against Australia.

Here, once again, he hit a wall of prejudice. Opposing his inclusion was none other than Lord Harris, Governor of Bombay from 1890 to 1895, then President of MCC, a former captain and a towering figure of authority and of the establishment. His Lordship thundered that only those 'native-born' should be eligible for England's Test side, ignoring the fact that he had been born in Trinidad, West Indies. It was a toxic combination of racism and double-standards, especially since Australian-born cricketers, including Sammy Woods, who had earlier represented their native countries in Test matches, had switched to representing England earlier that year.

Thus, Ranji was passed over for the first Test at Lord's, where Harris held sway. But with the hosting venue deciding the team, the Lancashire selectors had no hesitation in giving Ranji his debut at Old Trafford. Permission was sought from and granted by the Australian captain Harry Trott, whose brother Albert was to play for both Australia and then England.

The debut was nothing short of sensational. Though Australia won by three wickets, they came perilously close to losing, after enforcing the follow on, something that had befallen them for the first time just 18 months back in Sydney. Ranji became the second English batsman after his captain W.G. Grace to score a century on debut and the first Indian to play Test cricket. (The first Indian-born Test cricketer however was Australia's Bransby Cooper in the very first Test match versus England at Melbourne in 1877. He was born in Dacca, now Dhaka, then part of undivided India in 1844.)

The mighty fast bowler Tom Richardson captured 13 wickets in the match, but it was Ranji who kept the English batting flag flying with 62 in the first innings and a dazzling 154 not out in the second. That century, which happened on the third day, was the first instance of a batsman scoring a century before lunch. The legend of Ranji the batsman was now secure. And that place was cemented when he also scored a century in his first Test in Australia, a superb 175 in Sydney a year later. He topped the averages for England in that series.

It is worth noting here that Duleep also scored a century in his first Test against Australia, a splendid 173 in 1930, two years after his Test debut—only to be upbraided by his stern uncle in the pavilion for being careless in getting out! Duleep too suffered racism when he was dropped after his first Test against South Africa at Edgbaston in 1929. There are conflicting reports as to whether this was due to objections raised by the South African team management as they did not include non-whites in their teams and also did not appreciate playing against them, or whether it was due to the prejudice of senior officials in English cricket's establishment.

The uncanny coincidence of English royal debuts continued with the next, Iftikhar Ali Khan, the Nawab of Pataudi (Sr.), who marked his Test debut in the 1932–33 'bodyline' series with a century in the first Test at Sydney. The royal tradition continued in Indian Test cricket too. Iftikhar's son, Mansur Ali Khan, the former Nawab of Pataudi (Jr.) became the fourth member of the royal brigade to score a century versus Australia in his first Test against them, for India at Madras in 1964, this coming three years after his Test debut.

Duleep's nephew (sister's son) Hanumant Singh became the third royal to mark his Test debut with a century against England at Delhi in 1964. Two other members of the Nawanagar royal family played Test cricket for India, wicketkeeper K.S. Inderjitsinhji, who was Hanumant's cousin and, more recently, Ajay Daulatsinhji Jadeja, who played 15 Tests but excelled as a batsman and fielder in ODIs.

Going back to Ranji, the legend and the myth: in 1897, at the height of his fame, he published the seminal coaching book (with more than a little help from his cerebral friend and Sussex teammate C.B. Fry), *The Jubilee Book of Cricket*, released in the diamond jubilee year of the reign of Queen Victoria and 'dedicated, by her gracious permission, to Her Majesty the Queen-Empress'. In the final chapter 'Cricket and the Victorian Era', he begins:

> In the year of grace 1897 all the British Empire is joining together to congratulate her Gracious Majesty Queen Victoria upon the unparalleled duration of her reign. There is no part or condition of her loyal subjects' lives which may not fairly be called upon to prove its right to be

regarded as one of the blessings her Majesty may associate with her happy occupation of the throne of England.

The masterly—or cynical—manner in which Ranji parlayed his cricket exploits to lobby and influence the British government in his bid for the throne of Nawanagar was not lost on the hundreds of royal houses scattered across the length and breadth of pre-independent India.

Satadru Sen summed it up well: 'It is important to keep in mind that had Ranjitsinhji not played English games, he would never have become an Indian prince. He would, in all likelihood, have languished as a minor casualty of the politics of a minor Indian state.'[8]

The British support for his flimsy claims to the throne and the support he also got from Indian princes, notably Bhupinder's father Rajinder of the Royal House of Patiala, were a direct result of his sporting feats and fame. All those in positions of power back then, both British and Indian, were keen to rub shoulders with this cricket legend and even bend the rules for him. There are echoes of that trend till today in Indian society when it comes to celebrities in various fields, including cricket. They realized that the best way to the heart of the Empire was by playing and supporting that most English of games. Thus, Ranji indirectly saw to it that royal patronage was extended to cricket in India, which benefited countless players who were employed by the princes to play for their teams and often given military titles in the bargain. They also brought over legendary names from England and Australia to

---

[8]'Chameleon Games: Ranjitsinhji's Politics of Race and Gender', *Journal of Colonialism and Colonial History*, 2001. As quoted by Boria Majumdar in the chapter 'The Cricketing Jam', *Once Upon a Furore: Lost Pages of Indian Cricket.*

play and coach in the winter. Their patronage was not entirely altruistic. Apart from currying favour with the Crown, there was also ego and prestige involved, with royal XIs locked in fierce battle for the pride of their rulers. And while their support for cricket was invaluable, preceding government and later private sector (and now franchise) patronage of cricket in India, their machinations, politicking and ego tussles did incalculable harm to Indian cricket.

The Australian Dr Richard Cashman in his 1980 book *Patrons, Players and the Crowd: The Phenomenon of Indian Cricket*, highlighted this aspect in his book in the chapter 'The Indian Princes.'

There were those who suspected that much of the princely interest in cricket was due to political ambition or simply self-aggrandisment...It is difficult now to ascertain precisely why princes, like the Maharaja of Patiala (Bhupinder Singh), poured so much money into this game and why they competed with each other in the 1920s and 1930s for the controlling influence in Indian cricket. Whatever the particular motivation of the individual princes, there were clearly some social and political rewards which must have enhanced the keenness of competition for the top position in the cricket world. The holder of a high cricket office enhanced his social and political status with the British.

We have seen earlier in this chapter how Ranji helped and supported Amar Singh. Duleep too played a stellar role in India both just before and after independence, joining the Indian Foreign Service and being posted as India's first High Commissioner to Australia and New Zealand, an inspired choice since he had been a striking success on his only tour, of Australia and New Zealand in 1929–30. He was secretary of the Cricket Club of India, Bombay, and a national selector, chairman of the Public Services Commission of Saurashtra in 1954 and remained chairman of the All-India Council of Sports until his death in December 1959.

It must be acknowledged here that the House of Patiala (de Mello described Bhupinder as 'the father of Indian sport'), the Pataudis and the Gaekwads did a lot of good for Indian sport and cricket in particular, ulterior motives or not. At the other end of the scale were the likes of the notorious Pusapati Vijay Ananda Gajapati Raju, the maharaja of Vizianagram, perhaps the most undeserving Test cricketer of all time, who inveigled his wealth and politicking to ensure that he was made captain on the infamous 1936 tour of England. Vizzy's inflated ego, petty jealousies and machinations left an indelible stain on the name and reputation of Indian cricket. And he was far from the only toxic royal of his time.

It is a pity that the BCCI decided to institute the Vizzy Trophy for the inter-zonal university tournament. It is perhaps time that they gave a thought to renaming the Ranji Trophy too, after someone who played for and contributed to Indian cricket, unlike the English Test cricketer-prince.

Like so many royal figures, Duleep too suffered from poor health and died relatively young. Just as the BCCI announced the Ranji Trophy for the national championship, immediately after Ranji's passing in 1933, so it did with the Duleep Trophy zonal tournament on Duleep's death. Rodrigues also concedes, 'there is no doubt that Ranji's influence on Indian cricket was phenomenal and awe-inspiring. Ranji was a towering hero of Indian cricket in the bygone days and his successes inspired an entire generation of Indians to seek excellence in the willowy game and in life itself.'[9]

---

[9]Mario Rodrigues, *Batting for the Empire: A Political History of Ranjitsinhji,*

Cashman stresses the point that Ranji did promote cricket in India by his 'example'. He shared cricket coaches with other states and 'also assisted Indian cricket in small and often unnoticed ways'. (So small that they went unnoticed, compared to his munificence in England, Rodrigues adds in a sarcastic footnote in his book!)

Ranji was the first Indian to play Test cricket, albeit for England. But was he the first Indian cricket superstar? In fact, long before royalty had become enamoured with the game, it was the tiny but highly educated and wealthy Parsi Zoroastrian community who were the real pioneers of cricket of India.

The first cricket teams from India to sail overseas to play the noble game of cricket were the Parsis, who twice toured England, in 1886 and 1888. Though the first tour was a disaster, there was more success on the second and thus emerged the first real superstar of Indian cricket, the fast bowler Mehellasha Edulji Pavri. Back home, the Parsis handed out stinging defeats to the first three English teams to tour India.

Towards the end of the nineteenth century, there also emerged a masterly left-arm spinner who was a striking success in the first All-India tour of England in 1911. Baloo Palwankar, being a Dalit, overcame tremendous odds to make it to the Hindu team in the Bombay tournaments and then as the leading light of the disastrous 1911 tour.

That particular tour was the subject of an award-winning book by Prashant Kidambi in 2019, *Cricket Country: The Untold History of the First All India Team*, in which a few early myths of Indian cricket are put to rest in a thorough and brilliant manner. Kidambi debunks the line taken in numerous books and articles, that Ranji was an able administrator of Nawanagar

Penguin, 2003, p. 243

and did much to help develop its resources and support his subjects.

Having formally been installed as the new ruler of Nawanagar on 11 March 1907 in a ceremony in Jamnagar,

> very soon, Ranji's inadequacies as an administrator were exposed. Even as his state was simultaneously assailed by plague and drought, he devoted his energies to extracting more resources from his impoverished subjects. And like many of his princely peers, Ranji exercised his discretionary authority in a quixotic fashion. Morever, he quickly began to indulge his passion for luxury.

The other myth is that Bhupinder Singh, the newly appointed teenage Maharaja of Patiala, was instrumental in organizing the 1911 tour. This theory was even mentioned in a feature on the city of Patiala's cricket legacy in a national English daily dated 21 December 2019. The writer of the piece had obviously not read Kidambi's tome.

It was in fact the Parsi community who were at the forefront of this laudable venture. Largely funded by the famed Tata industrial family, it was J.M. Framjee Patel who worked diligently towards organizing the tour, earlier efforts having fallen through ostensibly due to lack of funds but also because of the various religious communities that were to make up the team, not seeing eye-to-eye. Patel was a former captain of the Parsi team and one of the organizers of the 1886 tour.

These efforts first began and failed in 1898 and then again in 1903; each time, Patel was determined to rope in Ranji as captain. But though he did not publicly commit one way or another, in keeping with his contempt for cricket in India, he was ridiculing the very idea of an Indian cricket team playing in England and helped scuttle the plans. As Kidambi notes, after his arrival in Bombay in December 1903, he gave a speech at the Parsi Ripon Club where a dinner had been organized in his honour, which was reported in *The Times of India* dated 25 January 1904.

The imperial cricketing superstar used the occasion to tear to shreds the idea of an Indian cricket tour of Britain. 'Why, Indian cricketers do not even know the ABC of the game, and an Indian team would find that in England there is no county so weak that it could not score 500 runs against Indian bowling and in turn dismiss the Indian team for 30 or 40 runs,' he scoffed.

This contemptuous attitude did not deter Patel and he continued to plead with Ranji in 1910, when the tour was finally given the green signal, to lead the side. Patel was convinced that there could not be anyone else who could fit the bill better than the legendary Maharaja of Nawanagar. Ranji of course declined, more politely this time and now to the surprise of many, the selection committee decided to ask the young prince Bhupinder to be captain.

Cashman[10] and earlier de Mello in their books both claimed the Maharaja of Patiala 'organized, financed, and captained (the 1911 tour).' Berry says the same in *Cricket Wallah*.[11]

In the chapter 'The Captain's Story', Kidambi effectively debunks this long-held view. Bhupinder's rule had come under intense scrutiny from the British authorities, alarmed as they were by his wayward behavior. 'Bhupinder had little time to devote to the cause of Indian cricket. Indeed, in the

---

[10]Richard Cashman, *Patrons, Players and the Crowd: The Phenomenon of Indian Cricket*, Orient Longman Limited, 1980, p. 32
[11]Scyld Berry, *Cricket Wallah: With England in India 1981-82*, Hodder & Stoughton, 1982, p. 47

eighteen months that went into the organization of the tour, the Maharaja's only tangible contribution was as a subscriber to the guarantee fund,' writes Kidambi.

Unlike the recalcitrant Ranji, Bhupinder pounced on the chance to go to England. It was the year of the coronation of King George V and the young prince was keen to rub shoulders with royalty and the cream of British society, while at the same time escaping the suffocating scrutiny over his rule back home. In the event, he played just three matches before leaving the tour early, due to health issues.

One enduring riddle concerning Ranji's private life is the question of why he never married. Being a lifelong bachelor was not considered proper for royalty, who were constrained to produce heirs to their throne, to continue the lineage after their passing.

Ranji's romantic links with Edith, one of the daughters of Reverend Louis Borissow, Ranji's tutor before entering Cambridge University, was no secret. De Mello hinted as such in his book when he wrote:

> Ranji's mind did not dwell amongst us in India. It was in England. And it is my understanding of this great and strange man that his heart was in England also...There was talk too of an unhappy love affair and certainly as an Indian prince Ranji could not marry an English girl.

What was not known till 2018 was that this romance with an English girl bore an illegitimate son, a scandal of immense proportions in the Victorian era, one that would have besmirched Ranji's reputation forever and scuttled his royal ambitions, as well as possibly driving him out of England.

This startling revelation appeared in the April 2018 issue of *Wisden Cricket Monthly*, but received very little publicity in

India. It was none other than Simon Wilde, the *Sunday Times* cricket correspondent and author of the 1990 book on Ranji, who broke the story after being contacted a few years earlier by Ranji's great-great-granddaughter, Catherine Richardson.

The son's name was registered as Bernard Kirk and the birth is thought to have occurred sometime in 1897. Wilde refers to the affair as 'a classic Establishment cover-up and a classic Victorian scandal', with the pregnant woman being hidden away and the boy soon given up for adoption, raised as Bernard Beardmore, his adoptive parents being Paul and Jane Beardmore. He died in 1976 aged 79, convinced all his life that he was Ranji's son. It was not known if Ranji had any contact with his son. Edith died in 1942 and also never married.

A hint at Ranji's state of mind was revealed by de Mello.

'Towards the end of his life, Ranji gave the impression that he was disillusioned. Always it seemed, he was waiting for something...' Was de Mello privy to this deepest of secrets of Ranji? And was that which 'he knew would he would never have', the son who he had been forced to abandon?

With Ranji's 150th birth anniversary (in 2022) just one year away, perhaps the myth of Ranji, the man and the legend, can finally be laid to rest.

Or can it?

Royalty in Test cricket (number of Tests in brackets)

For England
K.S. Ranjitsinhji of Nawanagar (15)
K.S. Duleepsinhji of Nawanagar (12)
Iftikhar Ali Khan, the Nawab of Pataudi Sr. (3)
Nasser Hussain of Arcot (96; 88 ODIs)

For India

Yadavendrasingh, Yuvraj of Patiala (1)

Pusapati Vijay Ananda Gajapati Raju, Maharajkumar of Vizianagram (3)

Iftikhar Ali Khan, the Nawab of Pataudi Sr. (3)

Kanwar Rai Singh of Patiala (1)

Dattajirao K. Gaekwad of Baroda (11)

Jaysinghrao M. Ghorpade of Baroda (8)

Mansur Ali Khan, the Nawab of Pataudi Jr. (46)

Hanumant Singh of Banswara (14)

K.S. Indrajitsinhji of Nawanagar (4)

Aunshuman D. Gaekwad of Baroda (40; 15 ODIs)

Yajurvindra Singh of Bilkha (4)

Ajay Jadeja of Nawanagar (15; 196 ODIs)

6

THE KD ERA, BEFORE AND AFTER

He came off the pitch like the crack of doom.

—Wally Hammond on Amar Singh

It was while travelling by tram on an October afternoon in 1978 in Calcutta, with the transistor as usual stuck to my ear, listening to the commentary from Faisalabad, that I turned round and relayed the startling news to my friends crowding around me and straining to listen in.

A teenager by the name of Kapil Dev opening the bowling for India in the opening Test of the series had forced Pakistan opener Sadiq Mohammed to call for—wait for it—a helmet!

There were two startling things about this incident. Firstly, even diehard cricket fans like me had barely heard the name of the debutant bowler before; secondly, an Indian bowler bowling with enough pace and fire to intimidate an opposition batsman was something we youngsters could only witness in our dreams.

Remember, this was the very first year helmets were being

worn in Test cricket (see Chapter 5). And it was also the first time since 1961 that India and Pakistan were meeting on a cricket pitch. So, there was enormous worldwide interest around the tour.

Kapil went wicketless in the first innings, though in the second Sadiq would become the first of his 434 Test wickets, in a storied career lasting 16 years. And among the most impressive of his stats is that he claimed 99 wickets against Pakistan on the heartbreaking tracks of India and Pakistan in 29 Tests, at the strike rate of 60.04. His ODI achievements were capped by leading India to an improbable victory in the 1983 Prudential World Cup, which changed the face of cricket forever in India and the world.

Like many youngsters who start off as tearaways, Kapil later cut down his pace and pragmatically concentrated on swing and length. In 2002, he was voted *Wisden Indian Cricketer of the Century*. It was a popular choice.

Today, when one witnesses the Indian fast bowling lineup knock over stumps and knock down batsmen, it's hard to imagine what it was like being an Indian cricket supporter in the 60s and 70s, when it was spin bowling and spin bowling alone that dominated Indian cricket.

We could only look with envy across the border at Pakistan's fast bowling attack led by the peerless Imran Khan. As for Australia and West Indies, well...! Indians, we were always told, just did not *do* fast bowling. All kinds of fanciful theories were trotted out for this. One coach at a national camp even taunted the young Kapil when he said that as a fast bowler he needed extra roti for stamina. 'There are no fast bowlers in India,' he was told mockingly.

Back then, we craved the sight of an Indian bowler troubling batsmen with pace and bounce. Kapil therefore was the answer to our dreams, and his opening partnership with left-armer Karsan Ghavri gave the Indian bowling real bite for the first time in living memory.

Inspired by his example, many followed in his wake, notably Javagal Srinath, Ashish Nehra, Manoj Prabhakar, Venkatesh Prasad, Zaheer Khan, S. Sreesanth and Praveen Kumar among others. The current generation of Mohammed Shami, Jasprit Bumrah, Ishant Sharma, Varun Aaron, Umesh Yadav, Jaydev Unadkat, Bhuvaneshwar Kumar, Shardul Thakur, Navdeep Saini and others have given the Indian captain today a luxury that his predecessors rarely enjoyed.

Or did they? Here is where myth and reality meet at the crossroads of Indian cricket history. So many today consider Kapil to be the first Indian pace bowler—before that it was only spin, spin and more spin, is the general impression about Indian cricket.

Sunil Gavaskar was spot-on at the 26th Lal Bahadur Shastri Memorial Lecture in New Delhi in January 2020 when he said, 'Kapil's greatest legacy was to show the budding Indian fast bowler that even on pitches without much assistance to them, they could take wickets. If India today has a cornucopia of fast bowlers, it is thanks to Kapil Dev.'

West Indies fast bowling veteran Ian Bishop, today one of the most intelligent of TV pundits, around the same time as Gavaskar, also stressed that it was Kapil who laid the foundation for today's all out pace attack. Bishop was one of those who terrorized Indian batsmen in the Caribbean in 1989, breaking opener K. Srikkanth's arm in the process. No wonder, he said that he could never have predicted that India's fast bowlers would come to the Caribbean and do to the West Indians what they did to others so many decades ago. Remember the nightmare Indian tours of West Indies in 1962, 1976, 1983,

1989...? (see Chapter 9)

But if Kapil Dev laid the foundation for today's generation of fast bowlers, who laid it for Kapil? Make no mistake that it is a myth that Kapil was the pioneer of pace bowling in India, though he undoubtedly remains the greatest by a country mile.

In fact, till Partition in 1947, Indian bowling largely revolved around fast bowling. The great left-arm spinner/all-rounder Vinoo Mankad, who made his Test debut in 1946, can be said to be the first great Indian spin bowler in Test cricket. (The left-arm spinner Baloo Palwankar did not get a chance to play Test cricket, though he was the outstanding bowler in the first All-India tour of England in 1911.)

Wrote Vijay Merchant in *Wisden Cricketers' Almanack* (1952):

> Above all, the partition has deprived India of future fast bowlers. In the past, India often relied for fast bowling on the Northern India people, who because of their height and sturdy physique, are better equipped for this kind of bowling than the cricketers of Central India or the South. Now this source of supply has ceased and the gap has not yet been filled.

While this may perpetuate stereotypes (Srinath, the fastest of modern Indian fast bowlers is after all from Karnataka), there is a grain of truth in what Merchant postulated.

When India played their maiden Test match at Lord's in 1932, it was the famous opening bowling pair of Mohammad Nissar and L. Amar Singh who rocked the mighty England batting in the first hour of play, leaving them reeling at 19 for three with Nissar—possibly the fastest Indian bowler of all time—knocking out the stumps of openers Herbert Sutcliffe and Percy Holmes.

Amar Singh's elder brother L. Ramji was also of express pace and was ruthless in his line of attack, terrifying batsmen from India, England and Australia, though he played just one official Test, in Bombay in 1933.

Nissar and Amar Singh were backed up by Jahangir Khan, father of Majid and uncle of Imran and, while Nissar captured five wickets in the first innings at Lord's, Jahangir got four of the eight to fall in the second—Holmes, Frank Woolley, Wally Hammond and Eddie Paynter. The trio were back in England in 1936 to lead the attack again and in between was the visit of Douglas Jardine's MCC/England side to India in 1933-34, plus tours to India of unofficial teams.

Amar died tragically young while Nissar and Jahangir both opted for Pakistan at Partition, by which time their careers were over in any case.

In *Sport and Pastime* (19 May 1962), S.K. Gurunathan wrote: 'Nissar was a giant in every sense of the word. He was tall, strong and sturdy and nature endowed him with ability to generate great pace off the pitch. He knew the art of swing.'

In the same article, he continued: 'It is just not an accident that Nissar, our best ever fast bowler, was born in the Punjab. Should another great fast bowler arrive, he would in all likelihood again be a Punjabi.'

Well, it happened 16 years later, and while Kapil was not a Punjabi, he is from Haryana, so close enough! Amar, incidentally, was from Gujarat.

However, the tradition of Indian fast bowling goes back even further, in fact to the late nineteenth century, and it was the pioneering Parsi community that produced the first great bowler of the kind, who was a striking success on their second tour of England in 1888.

The first tour two years earlier had been a disaster, but

there was considerable improvement on the next and this was largely thanks to the express bowling of Mehellasha Edulji Pavri (1866-1946) who took 170 wickets at the excellent average of 11.66 (Chapter 5).

Lillywhite's Cricketer's Annual of 1889 described him thus: 'He bowled fast round-arm of a good length, and towards the end of the tour developed a very good style, varying his pace and pitch well, besides making the ball do a good deal at times.'

It should be explained here that a number of the bowlers on the Parsi tours bowled underarm, as was the fashion then, but Pavri was an over-arm or round-arm bowler of considerable pace, whom cricket historian Vasant Raiji described as 'India's first great cricketer' (*India's Hambledon Men*), a massive frame and luxuriant beard giving him a fierce look.

Back home, the experience gained in England held the Parsis, and Pavri in particular, in good stead and they proceeded to inflict a string of stunning defeats on English cricketers in their backyard of Bombay, which fired up the imagination of their countrymen.

After crushing Bombay Gymkhana—made up entirely of Englishmen—by 10 wickets in September 1889, the Parsis continued their giant killing with a four-wicket victory over the first English team to tour India, led by Test cricketer G.F. Vernon in January 1890.

These were bitter pills for the British to swallow, even as the Parsis and fellow Indians jubilantly celebrated the crushing of their colonial masters. The British, on the other hand, were seething at these humiliations.

In a low-scoring match played over two days at Bombay Gymkhana, the English were all out for 97. The Parsis in turn collapsed for 82 and Vernon's XI then crashed in their second innings for 61, the Parsis losing six wickets before sealing their victory in front an ecstatic crowd of 10,000. Pavri was destroyer-in-chief, with figures of 13.2-5-34-7. His pace was simply too hot for the visitors.

This was the only defeat suffered on the tour by Vernon's team, and they ensured that there was no return fixture, such was their shock.

Less than three years later, cricket history was to repeat itself, with the Parsis once again triumphing against the next English team to tour, Lord Hawke's XI. And it was Pavri once again who struck terror in the hearts of the experienced Englishmen.

Hawke's team were routed by 109 runs, tumbling to 73 and 93 in their two innings, Pavri taking two wickets in the first innings and 6 for 36 in the second.

The glorious hat-trick was completed in November 1902 when the Parsis defeated the Oxford University Authentics by eight wickets on their favourite ground.

Pavri was now captain, but he took a back seat this time. In the grand Parsi tradition of fast bowlers, it was Ardeshir Mehta who took 6 for 97 in the first innings.

This Parsi team had in its ranks two fast bowlers, Maneksha Bulsara and K.B. Mistry who, by the turn of the century, had gained a reputation for speed and hostility. Bulsara earned the nickname of 'The Demon', after the legendary Australian fast bowler Fred Spofforth, though it was left-armer Mistry who earned the best figures of 9 for 81 in the Bombay Presidency match against the Europeans in Pune in the 1906–07 season.

Bulsara, though, was the more consistent of the two in the Presidency series of matches against the Europeans between 1892–93 and 1906–07. In only his second match in 1900–01, Bulsara had outstanding match figures of 13 for 52 (5-21 and 8-31) at Bombay, the Parsis winning by 135 runs as the Europeans collapsed for 51 and 82. In the final against the Europeans in the triangular tournament in 1907–08 (the Hindus being the other team), Bulsara had match figures of 10 for 50, as his team won by 143 runs. At his peak, he was considered the fastest Indian bowler.

Pavri told W.A. Bettesworth, author of *Chats on the Cricket Field*, that after the 1888 tour, he had learned how to vary his pace by watching the English Test fast bowlers Bill Lockwood and John Sharpe of Surrey. 'Lockwood was also good enough to show me how to make the ball break,' he explained.

Pavri played one match for Middlesex against Sussex at Hove in 1895, in which he came up against the great Ranji. He took only one wicket in the match. It is likely that it made him the first Indian cricketer to play county cricket, considering that Ranji was for all practical purposes an English cricketer (Chapter 5).

So, just as Kapil Dev in the twentieth century laid the foundation and inspired the generations that followed into the twenty-first century, so the nineteenth-century pioneers were to prove an inspiration for the generation of fast bowlers that put India on the world cricket map from the 1920s.

Nissar, Amar Singh and Jahangir Khan were all born in 1910 and they excelled in both official and unofficial Test matches. Ramji was born 10 years earlier (there is a dispute as to whether it was 1900 or 1902) and was past his peak by the time he played his lone Test in 1933.

A lesser-known figure in Indian cricket history, who later made a name for himself as a radio commentator, was Dev Raj Puri (born 1916), who had the misfortune of not being selected for the 1936 tour of England when at his peak. He was, according to Vijay Merchant, the fastest Indian bowler he had ever faced in his opening spell, and excelled both in the very first Ranji Trophy final for Northern Punjab in March

1935 as well as the first Rohinton Baria inter-collegiate final for Punjab University, Lahore in June 1936.

India has long been known as the land of spin, which is not surprising, considering that it has produced many all-time legends of spin bowling. But in the 1930s, the Indian psyche was more attuned to bowling fast.

At an official dinner for the 1933–34 English touring team at Amritsar, the lack of good spin bowlers in India was the topic of discussion between captain Douglas Jardine and Maharaja Bhupinder Singh of Patiala. Bhupinder's explanation for this was that Indians 'hate being laughed at. They say slow bowling means sixers, and fast or fast-medium stuff is seldom hit for six. So they won't practice slow bowling.'

Contrast this to how spin bowling was the dominant force in the 1960s and 70s and beyond.

While it was the blistering century by C.K. Nayudu against A.E.R Gilligan's MCC team of 1926-27 that made the headlines, it was Ramji who rocked and shocked the tourists in a two-day match at Ajmer, played on coir matting which assisted fast bowling.

Ramji took four wickets but bowled with such hostility that Gilligan feared for the lives of his batsmen, all hardened pros. He appealed to the rival captain, Lakshman Singh Bahadur, the Maharawal of Dungarpur, to take Ramji out of the attack and His Highness duly did so, leaving Ramji with figures of 23-1-81-4.

In the first unofficial Test at Bombay in December 1926, Ramji was the leading bowler with 7 of the 15 MCC wickets that fell in the drawn match.

On India's maiden Test tour in 1932, Nissar and Amar were a revelation to the English batsmen and spectators. Legendary English batsman Wally Hammond wrote of Amar in *Cricket*

My Destiny: 'He was as dangerous an opening bowler as I have ever seen, coming off the pitch like the crack of doom.'

It is measure of their skill and speed, that they were spoken of in the same breath as England's terrors Harold Larwood and Bill Voce of 'bodyline' fame and West Indians Manny Martindale and Learie Constantine, who gave the English a taste of their own medicine in 1933.

In 22 first-class matches on the 1932 tour, Amar Singh took 111 wickets in 22 matches while Nissar had 71 from 18. Despite losing by 158 runs in the one-off Lord's Test, it was the Indian's fast bowling that impressed the most. 'Onlooker' wrote in *The Cricketer* (2 July 1932): 'The bowling of Nissar, Amar Singh, Nayudu and Khan was really good. Loose balls were very seldom seen, and all the bowlers came fast off the ground. Nissar was the most successful but Amar Singh was probably the best.'

It was on the 1932–33 tour of Australia that Jardine unleashed Larwood and Co. on the home side, chiefly Don Bradman, to stanch the endless flow of runs from his bat. The 'bodyline' tactics were a danger to life and limb and hugely controversial, and though England won 4-1, it was not long before these tactics were outlawed.

Imagine Jardine's shock then, when he came to India the following season, and found his batsmen under threat from Ramji, Nissar and Amar. Such was his concern that he insisted all the batsmen—including himself—wear the sola topi or pith hat as an early form of protection. (Chapter 2)

England won two of the three Tests and Amar returned his best bowling figures of 7 for 86 in England's first innings in the third Test at Madras in February 1934. It would be 50 years before an Indian pace bowler bettered these figures.

There was more 'bodyline' style bowling from the Indians and this time it was Jack Ryder's motley team of Australian veterans and youngsters in 1935–36 who faced the music when they toured India for a series of four unofficial Tests. The series ended 2-2, with Nissar outstanding with 32 wickets.

Nissar was a gentle giant as far as his fellow Indians were concerned, against whom he refrained from bowling bouncers. Not so against foreigners and former Australian fast bowler Ron Oxenham (now 44), who complained in the *Brisbane Telegraph* (19 January 1936): 'Everyone has been hit by his "bumpers" and now that Wendell Bill is also a casualty, I am beginning to think it is time someone had a word with the Indian.'

Bill had his jaw broken by Nissar bowling for Patiala, the match played after the third unofficial Test at Lahore; he would never play another match again.

What was remarkable about the Lahore match in January 1936, which India won by 68 runs, was that the Indians went in with five pace bowlers—something unheard of for the next 82 years, till history repeated itself in the third Test at Johannesburg in January 2018. In Lahore, India fielded Nissar, Puri, 'Shute' Banerjee, Baqa Jilani and Amir Elahi (the last two, purveyors of both pace and spin).

The 1936 tour of England was overshadowed by controversy and bitterness, and though India lost two of the three Tests, the famed duo of Nissar and Amar once again covered themselves in glory. By now, they had established themselves as among the best in the world, and this reputation was only enhanced in the last international series they would bowl in together.

In 1937–38, the former England Test captain Lord Lionel Tennyson brought a strong team to play five unofficial Tests. It could be argued that it was the strongest to tour India till then, perhaps on par with Jardine's official team. Tennyson had played the last of his nine Tests back in 1921, but the 1937–38 team had in its ranks Alf Gover, Bill Edrich, Joe Hardstaff (Jr.),

Paul Gibb, Norman Yardley and Ian Peebles, all distinguished cricketers.

The Indians had never played five international matches in a series and it was topsy-turvy, the English winning the first two, the hosts storming back to win the next two, before running out of steam and losing the fifth and final and the series 3-2.

The visitors won the first two matches at Lahore and Bombay, India came back at Calcutta and Madras, before losing the fifth and final at Bombay. And it was Amar's sensational bowling on a damp pitch at Madras that saw India record their maiden innings victory in an international match, returning the sensational figures of 5 for 38 and 6 for 58, reaching the landmark of 450 first-class wickets in this match. He would finish with 506 from 92 wickets. Nissar had also taken 11 wickets in the fourth match at Madras against Ryder's Australian. The decider at Bombay was the last match in which the great pair opened the bowling together.

Every diehard Indian cricket fan knows that leg spin legend B.S. Chandrasekhar holds the record for most wickets in a Test series, 35 in the home series versus England in 1972–73, one more than the previous mark held by both Mankad and Subhash Gupte.

In fact, Amar grabbed 36 wickets in that 1937–38 series, the last international series played by India till the 1946 tour of England, due to the outbreak of World War II in 1939.

Amar's death at the age of 29 prompted *The Cricketer* (1 June 1940) to bemoan 'a great loss to cricket' and state that 'in selecting a World XI from present-day players, his claims would have been very seriously considered'.

The next generation of pace bowlers was led by C.R. Rangachari, the unfortunate Shute Banerjee, brilliant all-rounder Dattu Phadkar—the precursor to Kapil with his masterly outswing and an excellent batting record to boot—and the remarkable Ramakant Desai, who generated considerable pace from his frail frame and was nicknamed 'Tiny'. In the 1960–61 home series against Pakistan, Desai terrified their famed opener Hanif Mohammad, the original Little Master.

Desai made his debut in 1959 and played his last Test in 1968, just 28 Tests in all, as he was in and out of the team despite his fine record. But it was the 1960s and 70s (till the advent of Kapil in 1978), that were the barren years for Indian pace bowling.

A major reason for this was the pitches in domestic cricket, which were heartbreaking and backbreaking for anyone below express pace. It was 'Tiger' Pataudi who decided to go in for an all-spin bowling attack, making the opening couple of overs perfunctory, just to get the shine off the ball for the spin maestros to take over.

While Abid Ali, Eknath Solkar and Madan Lal picked up some useful wickets in their opening overs, many promising pace bowlers were left in the wake with the spin policy being the order of the day.

Chief among them was Maharashtra's Pandurang Salgaoncar, who was a terror in domestic cricket in the 1970s. He did play two unofficial Tests in Sri Lanka in 1974 with some success, taking seven wickets in the second unofficial Test at Colombo and bowling with pace and aggression. But the giant from Poona was hard done by when not chosen for the 1974 tour of England, despite being in peak form. Others like Abdul Ismail, Syed Ahmed Hattea and Kailash Gattani faced a similar fate.

Eventually came Kapil Dev, riding on the shoulders of the great fast bowlers of previous generations, and the face of modern Indian cricket was changed forever.

7

KAPIL'S 'STRIKING' INNINGS

*I was just going to stay there and
stick it out for the sixty overs.*

—Kapil Dev

On the face of it, England's South African-born batsman Basil D'Oliveira and India's dynamic all-rounder Kapil Dev do not appear to have much in common. In fact, both played innings of uncommon importance under immense pressure, which had domino effects that would lead to cataclysmic changes decades later.

'Dolly's' 158 in the fifth and final Test of the Ashes at the Oval in August 1968 (eventually) led to his selection for England's tour of South Africa, the apartheid government's refusal to allow him to play, their eventual ban from international cricket and their return in 1991 after the release from prison of Nelson Mandela after 27 years behind bars, the dismantling of the obnoxious apartheid system and finally, black majority rule in South Africa.

Kapil's 175 not against Zimbabwe at the Nevill Ground, Tunbridge Wells, Kent in the third Prudential World Cup in 1983 in England saved India from a precarious position, and almost certain exit from the event. It would lead to their passage to the semifinal after beating Australia in the next must-win group match. In the semis they would stun hosts England and then in one of the greatest upsets in the history of sport, dethrone twice-champions West Indies in the final at Lord's.

Though not in the same dramatic world-altering manner of Dolly's domino effect, Kapil's innings and the subsequent shattering events saw the World Cup leave England for the first time, move to the Asian subcontinent in 1987, heralding the end of the Anglo-Australian veto power in the International Cricket Council and the situation today where India—a bit player in world cricket pre-1983—is the 800-pound elephant in the room of world cricket. The victory in the inaugural ICC World T20 in South Africa in 2007 and the launch of the Indian Premier League a year later, only built on that amazing day at Tunbridge Wells.

The myths surrounding the third World Cup are myriad and mystifying, and the first of these is that India were no-hopers going into the event.

They were rank outsiders and, going by their abysmal record in the first and second Prudential World Cups in England in 1975 and 1979, it was easy to dismiss them out of hand as some experts did in their preview pieces.

However, this ignored the fact that by the start of the decade, India had in fact notched up some notable wins in ODIs, in India, Australia, Pakistan and West Indies.

India's first victory against a Test playing nation in an ODI came at Quetta in the 1978 tour of Pakistan. In 1980–81, in the second season of the Benson and Hedges World Series triangular tournament in Australia, India started with a bang by winning three of their first five matches, one against Australia and two against New Zealand, before fading out and failing to make the finals. But the tournament taught the inexperienced Indians many valuable lessons in the format, which they then brought to the fore when the first ODIs were staged on Indian soil in 1981–82. India beat the far more experienced England 2-1 for their first series victory.

The 1982–83 season, in the run up to the World Cup, saw India whitewash Sri Lanka 3-0 at home, win a match in Lahore on the last day of 1982 and then, three months later, came the match that should have opened the eyes of the experts both in India and abroad, who so contemptuously dismissed India's chances in the World Cup that followed.

Surprise at Berbice

It was at the Albion Sports Complex in Berbice, Guyana on 29 March 1983 that India recorded the highest total by any side against the reigning world champions, 282 for 5 in 47 overs (reduced from 50 by the hosts' slow over rate), considered a mammoth total for that era.

There was consistent batting down the order, with opener Sunil Gavaskar laying the foundation with 90 from 117 balls. Kapil's 'astonishing assault' (72 from 38 balls) in the words of Bill Frindall in *Limited-Overs Cricket: The Complete Record* saw him reach his 50 from 22 balls.

The captain then took the wickets of Gordon Greenidge and Andy Roberts, conceding 33 runs in his 10 overs for the Man of the Match award. Vivian Richards raced to 64 from 51 balls, hammering Madan Lal for seven fours off his first

10 fours in reaching 50, but in an ominous sign of things to come, it was Madan who got the prized wicket. And speaking of ominous signs (for West Indies that is), India's 'Swinging Sikh' Balvinder Singh Sandhu bowled opener Gordon Greenidge for a duck in the second Test at Port of Spain, Trinidad.

Berbice is the hometown of Rohan Bholalall Kanhai and, writing for the *Indian Cricketer* magazine (May 1983), he described the win by 27 runs as a 'nearly unbelievable achievement'. Auspiciously, it was played on Holi, which is known in Guyana as Phagwah Day and the ground was packed with cheering 'East Indian' supporters.

In his autobiography *Straight from the Heart*, Kapil was unequivocal:

> I can say with absolute conviction that we won the Prudential World Cup 1983 solely because we got this chance to play the West Indies, winners of the previous two World Cups, just before the showpiece event is to begin in England in June 1983, i.e. barely a month after the five-Test series in the Caribbean...Not a soul seriously believes that we would turn the world upside down by winning the Prudential World Cup; but we are certainly more optimistic...

India's World Cup campaign began with a bang. Berbice was repeated at Old Trafford, Manchester and the reigning champions thus were defeated for the first time in a World Cup match. Still, the experts shrugged it off as an aberration.

It was the 200th ODI and the Man of the Match was Yashpal Sharma with 89. For years, Yashpal sought a video of the match. Unfortunately for him and for cricket history, there was no telecast. But more on that later.

The opening day of the World Cup also saw another major

upset with 1975 runners-up Australia being shocked by Cup debutants Zimbabwe, their entire playing XI in fact making their ODI debuts. Captain Duncan Fletcher, who was to make a name for himself as a coach decades later, was Man of the Match.

The World Cup had got off to a rollicking start on June 9, with the eight teams divided into two groups, each playing each twice and the top two from each group advancing to the semifinals. Two days after their opening match, India beat Zimbabwe, but then were beaten by Australia and West Indies in the return match.

So, when India and Zimbabwe squared up again on Saturday, 18 June it was a do-or-die match for the Indians. Australia was level with India on points but had a superior run rate. So to make the next game against Australia a virtual semifinal, India had to beat the Zimbabweans while improving their run rate.

That meant if India won the toss, they would have to bat first and put up a big total. The toss was won and India did take first strike, despite Kapil's misgivings as the pitch was damp and would aid Zimbabwe's canny seamers.

The task of keeping track of the run rate was in the hands of famed cricket journalist R. Mohan of *The Hindu* from Madras. Mohan had travelled the cricket world with the team and was particularly close to Kapil, who sought his advice on what to do in the event of winning the toss and Mohan told him to bat first.

Apart from Mohan, the other Indian print journalists present were freelancers G. Viswanath, Ayaz Memon and Marathi journalists Pappu Sanzgiri, Yashwant Chad and the late Chandrasekhar Sant. There were also two freelance photographers, both from Calcutta, Srenik Sett and the late

Amiya Tarafdar.

Mohan told me that he was the only one who arrived before the start of the match, as he was driven to the ground by the late Bombay-born, London-based Dickie Rutnagur, while the rest had to catch trains from London. They thus missed the dramatic opening minutes as India crashed to 9 for 4.

Mohan (in an email dated 14 November 2019) said that when he advised Kapil to bat first because of the run rate issue, Kapil responded, '*Wicket to thoda geela hai.*' (The wicket though is a bit damp.) 'I immediately said that the decision after the toss would be his alone. If only he had put them in, they wouldn't have made 100.'

> I was s****ing in my pants when Kapil walked in at 9 for 4. His habit of looking up at the sun when going in to bat brought me and him in perfect eye contact, as the press box window was right above the entrance and below the pavilion clock. I thought I had screwed it up for India and didn't even eat lunch. Then Kapil played all those brilliant shots after lunch into the rhododendron bushes and the rest, as they say, is history.

History indeed! But when the fifth wicket fell at 17 in the 12th over, the only thing on the captain's mind was to play himself in. He had walked in at 11.18 a.m., and was determined to stay till the end, which he achieved when the innings closed at 2.20 p.m. After the fall of the fifth wicket, he wrote in *Sportsworld* (29 June 1983): 'I said to myself, I was just going to stay there and stick it out for the sixty overs.'

This was after all the third (and last) 60-overs World Cup, so time was on his hands and now it was the responsibility of the lower order to hang in and give Kapil the support he so desperately needed.

With Madan Lal for support, the total had crawled to 106 for 7 from 35 overs, with Kapil on 51. The 100 came from 100 balls and it was only after that, with wicketkeeper Syed Kirmani (the next highest scorer with 24) for company, he began smashing the bowlers to all parts and the final 75 runs of that remarkable knock took just 38 balls and fours and sixes rained around across the picturesque ground.The unbroken ninth wicket stand of 126 was a world record and by the end India had scrambled home by 31 runs.

Only the few thousand present at the ground have ever witnessed that remarkable innings and only their memories will keep it alive, as there was no telecast and hence no recording. As Kapil told Rajdeep Sardesai in his book *Democracy XI: The Great Indian Cricket Story*: 'I guess I could have shown it [the video] to my grandchildren, now they will have to read the scorecard.'

The BBC Strike that Wasn't

The story though that there was no live telecast because BBC were on strike that particular day, remains one of the great myths of the Prudential World Cup.

In fact, such was the manic schedule that the entire tournament was completed in just 16 days, with four group matches packed into one day. BBC had been on strike intermittently through the sporting summer and many major events, including the prestigious Royal Ascot horse race, were not shown live as a result. But there was no strike on that Saturday and the evidence lies in the live telecast of two games on that day, England versus Pakistan and Australia versus West Indies, the latter of which was also broadcast in Australia.

BBC back then in fact had just two channels and, apart

from England's matches, the producers had to take a call on one other to be telecast. India, considered rank outsiders right till their final group match when they made the semifinals, were just not considered big enough to merit such consideration. A far cry indeed from the modern age, when India's television deals are the lifeblood of world cricket. In fact, just one of India's group games was telecast live and this was the first one against Australia at Trent Bridge, Nottingham on 13 June, which India lost by 162 runs.

The myth of the BBC strike has been repeated ad nauseam over the decades in countless articles and books, including Kapil Dev's autobiography and Balvinder Singh Sandhu's book *The Devil's Pack: The Men Behind the '83 Victory* where he writes: 'It is indeed sad that this epic inning (sic) was not recorded for posterity, as BBC TV was on strike that day.'

As he walked back unbeaten on 175, a new world ODI record, Gavaskar met him halfway with a glass of water saying, 'Kapil, bad luck yaar.'[12]

> 'I assure him, "Well, the score is all right. We can still fight..." And he explains he's referring to the fact that there's no television coverage. "What a loss, man! We are the only lucky ones who have seen one of the most memorable innings. What a pity." Sadly so, since the BBC is on strike with some problem within the organization and our game is sacrificed.'

Team manager P.R. Man Singh writes in his book *Victory Insight: A Manager's Diary for the 1983 and 1987 World Cup*, that in the evening news, BBC showed footage of Kapil batting from the Test series held in England the previous year, thus

---

[12]From *Straight from the Heart* by Kapil Dev

proving once again that there was no BBC strike, since the evening news bulletin was on. Man Singh also confirmed to me that the BBC simply decided India's group matches (save for one) were not worth telecasting. He also touches on the urban myth circulating in the 1980s, that Kapil had paid a private cameraman to record the match and was selling tapes at rupees one lakh each, a princely sum back then!

Nikhil Naz notes in *Miracle Men: The Greatest Underdog Story in Cricket*:

> There aren't any cameras at the ground to relay live pictures. None to record it for a highlights package later. The BBC has two very sumptuous cricket matches on its menu already. The broadcaster's programme for the day reads: 'The four most powerful cricketing countries in the world do battle. WEST INDIES meet AUSTRALIA at Lord's, and Old Trafford [England v Pakistan] will witness a vital result with only one match remaining before the semifinals. Commentators: Old Trafford: RICHIE BENAUD; TONY GREIG; FRANK TYSON; Lord's: JIM LAKER, TOM GRAVENEY, TED DEXTER.

B. Sreeram, an avid cricket researcher based in Chennai, also unearthed the same listings as above from the morning newspapers of 18 June. In *The Times* TV listings for the day, shown to me by Australian cricket statistician Lawrie Colliver, apart from the telecast of the two matches on BBC 1 and BBC 2, it is also mentioned 'plus the latest scores of the New Zealand versus Sri Lanka match, and the India versus Zimbabwe match.' Significantly, there is no mention of the highlights of these two matches being shown on TV.

In addition, Sreeram has also sourced a report from the *Glasgow Herald* dated Monday, 20 June 1983 which reveals the strike which had continued through the summer had been lifted on that very day, the first day of Wimbledon. 'Wimbledon tennis was among several major events threatened by the dispute this week. Others include the State Opening of Parliament and the Queen's Speech on Wednesday, and the remaining matches of the Prudential World Cup cricket, culminating in the final at Lord's on Saturday.' To think if the dispute between BBC and the unions over daily allowance for staff had not been settled in time, the final at Lord's on 25 June would not have been telecast!

The report also states: 'Disruption [in telecasts] has already meant that the BBC lost coverage of Royal Ascot, two world cup matches, and the finals of tennis from Eastbourne,' but it does not specify which two matches were not telecast.

The Nevill ground itself has become a sort of a pilgrimage site for Indian cricket fans and during the 2019 ICC World Cup held in England, two journalists, Kushan Sarkar of PTI and K.C. Vijaya Kumar, sports editor of *The Hindu* both visited the venue to meet some of those who had witnessed the legendary innings, as they tried to recreate some of the magic of that day.

Kumar in his article dated 21 June 2019, wrote that a member of the 1983 squad (unnamed) once told him: 'I think the strike was an excuse, the BBC presumed that there no value in reporting a game involving India and Zimbabwe.'

Of course, as we have seen, it was not an excuse, it was merely because with just two channels, BBC had to decide which of the four daily matches were to be telecast. And the choice they made that day was logical under the circumstances.

Twist in the Tale

But there is a twist in the tale of the BBC strike, and it comes in the form of Mohan's comments in a feature on all-rounders for a *Sportstar* World Cup special, prior to the 1996 Wills World Cup.

In the issue dated 5 January 1996, Mohan writes of *that* innings at Tunbridge Wells: 'The men of BBC were on strike then and one or two cameramen who were there before the start also decided to wind up for the day. Hence, there is no video record of what was easily the most astonishing one-day innings.'

I got in touch with Mohan to verify this and he replied on 28 January 2020 that, as he and Rutnagur were driving to the ground around 10 a.m., an hour before the start of the match, they met the two cameramen who were known to Rutnagur and they briefly stopped at the entrance to the ground and told him that due to the BBC strike called that morning, they were leaving the ground.

When I mentioned to Mohan that two matches were telecast live on that day, his theory was that there was perhaps a strike in the news division to which these two were attached and the live telecasts were not affected or were 'beyond the pale of that strike', as he put it.

However, Man Singh writes in his book about watching the evening news, as already mentioned in this chapter, in which they showed old footage of Kapil batting. In fact, English cricket followers and journalists have told me that apart from the two matches out of four every day in the group stage, there were no highlights of the other two games shown on BBC, either as a package or even snippets on the evening news bulletins.

I reached out to Nick Hunter through his son Neil Hunter, Director, Sky News. Hunter senior had been, at the time, Executive Producer of BBC Sport in charge of cricket and also OB (Outside Broadcast) Director. In an email, Neil told me that his father did not 'remember much' of the details surrounding the coverage of the match. He did however state that the minimum number of cameras needed to telecast a match back then was three and Mohan confirmed that he and Rutnagur met two leaving the ground.

Veteran Kent-based freelance cricket writer Mark Baldwin confirmed to me that Tunbridge Wells had a local BBC station and conjectures that the two cameramen would have been at the ground to capture a couple of minutes of highlights/ interviews for the local evening news, as it was the first time the Nevill ground was staging an ODI.

The fact that Mohan saw them carrying away their cameras also proves that there were no 'fixed' cameras at the ground, which would have been required for telecasting the entire match or even a highlights package.

In conclusion, one can surmise that the technicians' strike, which was on and off through the summer, may have partially affected some of the regional (but not national) channels on that particular day and in a sort of 'go-slow', those two cameramen were recalled before the start of play.

What is beyond a shadow of doubt is that two matches were telecast live on BBC 1 and BBC 2 and even if there had been a clip shown on the Tunbridge Wells local channel, it is likely to have been a few seconds at most of Kapil's monumental innings.

The Phantom Catch

India started the tournament at 66-1 odds, and those rose to 100-1 during the break between the innings in the final against West Indies at Lord's on 25 June.

A total of 183 all out was just hopeless against the mighty Windies batting, led by the peerless Viv Richards, one of four in the side playing their third successive final. A hat-trick was surely on the cards for the 1975 and 1979 champions. Fast bowler Malcolm Marshall had even put down a non-refundable deposit on a swanky new car on the eve of the final with the prize money he was so confident of winning.

Anchoring the final from the Doordarshan studios in New Delhi, Dr Narottam Puri told the Indian viewers watching on TV, 'India can kiss the World Cup goodbye.'

He was hardly alone in his pessimism. Watching at home in Madras, I turned to my brother Jawahar and despairingly told him that perhaps the sheer willpower of 500 million Indians will win the day. He could only smile wanly. In the *Indian Express* office where I worked, on duty was the night sub, late Rayan Amal Raj. He confessed to us the next day that he had decided at the break what his headline for the match report would be: 'Gone with the Windies'.

Back home, we watched in wonder as opener Greenidge (1) shouldered arms to a seemingly innocuous delivery from Sandhu—which nipped back and removed the bails. Five for one after two overs. Shortly after, came a break in the telecast. This was no 'sorry for the break' moment which DD was so notorious for, because of technical glitches. The break had been announced beforehand. But what was the reason for it? I had a vague recollection but, to jog my memory, I spoke to Dr Puri.

He was not sure of the duration or the cause, but recalls going to eat at the Hotel Kanishka coffee shop not far from the DD studios. He then put me on to S.S. Bhakoo, who had recently retired as senior producer and was on the production team for the final. Bhakoo told me the break in transmission was due to 'sun outage', which causes an interruption in or distortion of the satellite signal. And as a result of the outage, millions in India were deprived of the most dramatic passage in play, when the champion's top order crumbled, after which the telecast resumed.

All cricket fans switched to the BBC World Service radio commentary and listened in mounting disbelief as one big-name batsman followed another back to the pavilion. The result—no one in India watched the iconic catch by Kapil Dev which signaled the end of the brief but brutal onslaught of Master Blaster Richards. Madan Lal had removed Desmond Haynes and despite a pasting in his previous over, he was back to take the prized wicket.

Nikhil Naz in his book and also Tom Alter and Ayaz Memon in their jointly authored book *The Best in the World: India's Ten Greatest World Cup Matches*, mention the break in the telecast, though the latter gets the timing wrong. The telecast did not miss the start of the innings and also did not resume after the fall of the second wicket as stated in *The Best in the World*. It happened after the fall of Greenidge and was off for over an hour. And so, they could not have watched Richards' dismissal, which came at 57 for three. No one in India could have watched that dismissal for that matter, as both Dr Puri and Bhakoo have confirmed. Naz rightly narrates that DD had recorded a concert of Mohamed Rafi to fill the gap in the transmission. One of the biggest moments in Indian cricket history and no live pictures!

It was not till much later, when the video eventually wound its way to India, that cricket lovers were able to marvel at the athleticism and calm of Kapil and his wondrous catch.

Oddly, writer Mukul Kesavan and some others too have recounted vividly their emotions on watching the catch live on their TVs in India. Kesavan wrote in *Cricinfo* magazine (April 2007) of watching the dismissal on the new colour TV of a friend and, in the same year, in his book *Men in White: A Book of Cricket*, in the chapter on Kapil Dev, this is how he described the catch:

> I can still see him catching Viv Richards off Madan Lal
> in that World Cup final: he loped off after the ball and
> collected it over his shoulder. It was a tough catch at a
> tense time in the biggest arena in cricket, but he made it
> look simple with his easy athleticism and Br'er Rabbit smile.

Soumya Bhattacharya, in the first chapter ('Just Where Were You When it Happened?') of *All That You Can't Leave Behind: Why We Can Never Do Without Cricket,* writes how he had given up on the game and was at a neighbourhood restaurant in Calcutta to pick up dinner, when he heard the Richards dismissal on the radio 'and by the time I returned home...West Indies was 66 for 5. The unbelievable was happening in front of our eyes—on the new black-and-white TV.'

Rajdeep Sardesai was fortunate enough to be present at Lord's that glorious summer day. So, he too can be forgiven for writing in his book: 'The catch (off Richards) and the image of Kapil Dev lifting the cup are embossed in my memory because they were among the first "live" moments captured on colour television in India.'

Yes, we witnessed the lifting of the cup—but not the catch, which so many claim to this day on social media!

Bowlers on Top

The term 'bits-and-pieces' cricketer has acquired negative connotations on social media, but back in 1983, it was a term that was widely accepted in describing some of those who played a leading role in India's Prudential Cup triumph.

Among them were all-rounders Roger Binny and Madan Lal, neither with exceptional international records, except for the World Cup. The conditions in England suited their gentle swing bowling and indeed they excelled in England in 1986 too, when India won the Test series 2-0.

Mohinder Amarnath—bowling at an even gentler pace— and Sandhu were in a similar mould, though Kapil Dev was in a different class altogether. He topped the batting averages for India at the World Cup, and was third in the bowling averages with 12 wickets, behind Madan Lal (17 wickets; average 16.76) and Roger Binny, the topper in the tournament with 18 wickets (average 18.67).

In an interview by photographer Srenik Sett with Vivian Richards in the *Indian Cricketer* (July–August 1983), the West Indian master, when asked to single out someone from the Indian team, plumped for Binny: 'The name that immediately comes to mind is Roger Binny. He was the most consistent performer in the Indian side throughout the tournament. Super performance by this lad.'

Joint second with Madan Lal was Sri Lanka's medium pacer, 24-year-old Ashantha de Mel, with 17 wickets at the outstanding average of 15.59 in just six matches—both Binny and Madan Lal having played two more. However, the Sri Lankans have asserted ever since that De Mel was joint top wicket-taker. How so? See the letter below that was published in the September 1983 issues of the English cricket magazines *The Cricketer* and *Wisden Cricket Monthly*.

In the run up to the 2019 ICC World Cup, I posted this letter on Twitter and a discussion ensued as to whether the assertion by the Lankan manager (since deceased) was enough to alter the records. Lawrence Booth, the current editor of *Wisden Cricketers' Almanack*, felt that it was: ('that letter seems pretty conclusive', was his comment on Twitter on 5 May 2019). However, he was alone in that opinion and even as *Wisden* gives De Mel's analysis in the match in question as 9-2-35-3 and Rumesh Ratnayake's as 11-0-55-0, *all* other books, magazines and websites give the analysis as 8-2-30-2 and Ratnayake as 12-0-60-1.

One more for de Mel

IN the match between Sri Lanka and New Zealand played at Bristol, Geoff Howarth was caught by Madugalle off Ashantha de Mel. Unfortunately, the scorers, who were assisted in identification of Sri Lankan players by a Sri Lankan who was not a member of our official

De Mel: superb World Cup.

squad, recorded in the score book that the bowler was Ratnayake and not de Mel. This was brought to my notice late last week and after enquiring from Duleep Mendis, from Madugalle the fielder, and Ratnayake the bowler to whom the wicket had been awarded incorrectly, I have satisfied myself that Ashantha de Mel was the bowler.

I am bringing these facts to your notice so that any official records maintained in respect of the World Cup Tournament may be altered accordingly. Rectification of this error results in de Mel sharing with Roger Binny of India the honour of being the leading wicket taker and besides, de Mel's average of 14.72 places him third in the bowling averages behind Richard Hadlee and Malcolm Marshall.

T. MURUGASER
(Manager, Sri Lanka Cricket Squad 1983)

Photo courtesy: The Cricketer (UK), September 1983

The extra five runs and extra wicket would mean De Mel's average would be exactly 15—18 wickets for 270. The manager Murugaser in his letter has not factored in these five extra runs, which have been added to De Mel's figures as that one over purported to have been bowled by Ratnayake, in which Howarth's wicket was claimed and one over of De Mel have been swapped by *Wisden*.

The doyen of cricket statisticians, the late Bill Frindall had this to say about the issue in his *The Wisden Book of One-Day Internationals 1971-1985*:

> Five weeks after the match was played, T. Murugaser, manager of the Sri Lankan team, wrote to the secretary of the TCCB [Test and County Cricket Board, organizers of the Prudential World Cup], announcing that Howarth was dismissed off the bowling of De Mel. As no such comment was made by the Sri Lankan captain [Duleep Mendis] when handed the bowling figures at the end of the New Zealand innings, and as both scorers were adamant that they had identified the bowler correctly, the original version is expected to be correct.

The match was played on 13 June and was not telecast, so highlights were not recorded. Of the four matches played on that day, there was a live telecast of England versus Pakistan and India versus Australia. West Indies versus Zimbabwe was the fourth game of the day.

A thorough search of the records has also failed to locate a photo of the dismissal of Geoff Howarth. So what do the three players involved have to say?

Ranjan Madugalle, the fielder in question, is now an ICC Match Referee and perhaps felt it was best to play safe. In an email reply to me dated 23 December 2019, he wrote:

'Unfortunately, I have no clear memory of this incident at all now. Sorry for not being of any help to you on this.'

There was no doubt in the minds of either De Mel or Ratnayake though when I got in touch with them by email. Ratnayake, Lanka's bowling coach, in an email dated 31 December 2019, wrote: 'One of his [De Mel's] wickets has come to me accidentally, as you have mentioned. Please do the necessary adjustments and notify the right sources to sort this error.'

Cricketer Asia (October 1983), in its statistical round-up of the World Cup, carried this box item:

> Correction: It's been officially announced that in Sri Lanka's first match against New Zealand, Asantha de Mel had bowling figures of 3-30 and Rumesh Ratnayake didn't get any wicket. Thus De Mel ended the competition with 18 wickets, the same as India's Roger Binny!

Sri Lanka won only one of their six group matches, against New Zealand in the return match at Derby, where de Mel was the chief destroyer with 5 for 32, as Lanka won by three wickets. He also took five wickets against Pakistan at Headingley, with Lanka losing by 11 runs.

De Mel was the only bowler in the tournament with two five-wicket hauls. But was he joint top wicket-taker with Binny, with 18 wickets, or joint second with Madan Lal with 17? Until a photograph appears, clearly showing the bowler in the Howarth dismissal, this will remain one of the abiding myths *and* mysteries of the 1983 Prudential World Cup.

Varying emotions at the end of the second tied Test match in cricket history at Madras in 1986. Bowler Greg Matthews is chased by ecstatic Australian teammates; Indian batsmen Maninder Singh and Ravi Shastri look stunned by umpire Vikram Raju's decision.

Photo by: Kamal Julka

Former Bengal and East Zone captain, Raju Mukherji, with mini bats signed by both the Indian and Australian 1986 tied Test teams.

Photo courtesy: Seema Mukherji

Sankaran Srinivasan with Allan Border, Australia's captain in the 1986 Madras tied Test at the Sydney Cricket Ground in January 2019.

Photo courtesy: Sankaran Srinivasan

Sunil Gavaskar tries on his skullcap for the first time at the Buchi Babu Tournament, Madras, August 1983.

Photo by:
S. Kothandaraman, The Hindu Images.

Film critic Saibal Chatterjee with the *Lagaan* poster.

Photo courtesy: Saibal Chatterjee

Ravi Shastri after hitting Baroda bowler Tilak Raj (background) for the sixth six in the over with non-striker Ghulam Parkar also in the photo, Bombay, January 1985.

Photo by: Thomas Rocha, The Hindu Images

Non-striker Bill Brown turns round to see bowler Vinoo Mankad remove the bails and run him out in the second Test at Sydney, December 1947. The umpire is Andrew Barlow, batsman is Arthur Morris and wicket-keeper is J.K. Irani.

Photo courtesy: Rahul Mankad

Ranji and nephew Duleep as depicted on Will's cigarette cards.

From author's personal collection

Author and historian Ramachandra Guha by the statue of Vinoo Mankad, Jamnagar, December 2012.

Photo courtesy: Ira Guha

Wife Romi greets Kapil Dev after he became the world record hold for
most Test wickets, Ahmedabad, February 1994.

Photo by: Kamal Julka

India's first great Test opening bowling pair of Mohammad Nissar (left)
and Amar Singh.

Photo courtesy: Waqar Nissar

The Nevill Ground, Tunbridge Wells, Kent in 2019.
Photo courtesy: Kushan Sarkar

1983 Prudential World Cup final: Kapil Dev is mobbed by ecstatic teammates after *that* catch to dismiss Viv Richards off Madan Lal (left). Top scorer K. Srikkanth is also visible.

Photo courtesy: Martin Williamson

1983 Prudential World Cup final: West Indies' first wicket falls, opening batsman Gordon Greenidge bowled by Balvinder Singh Sandhu for 1. Srikkanth, Kapil Dev, Kirmani and Gavaskar are the fielders.

Photo courtesy: Martin Williamson

Another six from Kapil Dev during his epochal 175 not out v Zimbabwe
at Tunbridge Wells, Prudential World Cup 1983.

Photo by: Srenik Sett

1983 Prudential World Cup final: The final wicket falls, Michael Holding lbw Mohinder Amarnath.

Photo courtesy: Martin Williamson

The photo of Nari Contractor with infant son Hoshedar

Photo courtesy: Hoshedar Contractor

Moments before Sadanand Vishwanath stumped Javed Miandad off L. Sivaramakrishnan, Benson & Hedges World Championship of Cricket final. March 10, 1985, MCG.

Photo courtesy: Cricket Victoria

The Indian team celebrates with the Benson & Hedges World Championship of Cricket Trophy. Melbourne, March 10, 1985.

Photo courtesy: Cricket Victoria

Salim Durani with legendary actress the late Parveen Babi and director B.R. Ishara (centre) on the sets of the Hindi movie *Charitra* in 1973.

Publicity still

An emotional Sunil Gavaskar greets Salim Durani on the opening day of the inaugural India/Afghanistan Test match. Bengaluru, June 14, 2018.

Abbas Ali Baig on the receiving end of that famous kiss, Bombay, January 1960.

Farokh Engineer (right) with his first Test captain Nari Captain during a Parsi cricket tournament at the Gymkhana grounds in Secunderabad on January 16, 2012.

Photo by: V. V. Subrahmanyam/The Hindu Images

8

TRAUMA IN PARADISE

It was like war.

—Bishan Singh Bedi

The tour to West Indies in 1976, under the captaincy of Bishan Singh Bedi over four Tests, remains one of the most dramatic in cricket history.

It was also the series that set the template for West Indies' world domination over the next two decades, which ended only in 1995 when West Indies surrendered the Sir Frank Worrell Trophy at home to Australia, the trophy which had been at stake in the Test series between the two teams since the 1960s. And it has been downhill almost all the way since.

Under Clive Lloyd's captaincy, West Indies won the World Cup in England in the first two editions in 1975 and 1979, before being shocked in the 1983 final by India. They have not reached a World Cup final since.

So, what made that 1976 series stand out?

First, let us look at the background. After their victory in the inaugural World Cup, following a 3-2 series win in India in 1974–75, Lloyd's men were riding the crest of a wave as they toured Australia in 1975–76, in what was billed as the unofficial world Test championship.

However, the series ended in a drubbing for West Indies, as Australia's pace attack, combined with hostile crowds and poor umpiring, saw Windies blown away 5-1 by Greg Chappell's Australians.

The pace attack of Dennis Lillee, Jeff Thomson, Max Walker and Gary Gilmour heaped injury and insult on a batting line up that had dominated both the World Cup final and group match against the same Aussies at Lord's in the summer of '75.

West Indies cricket was thus in crisis and Lloyd's brief tenure as captain was on the line, when the series against India began in 1976. The home side had it easy in the opening Test at Bridgetown, Barbados but then India almost turned the tables in the second at Port of Spain, Trinidad. The first day's play was washed out and by the end of the match, the visitors had much the better of the draw.

The third Test was to be staged at Georgetown, Guyana, but torrential rain saw the venue switch back to Port of Spain, which traditionally favoured spinners For the first and only time in their storied history, Lloyd went in with three specialist spinners but they all failed and India set a new world record as they scored 406 for 4 to record a famous victory. That's when the all-out fast bowling attack that decimated opposing sides for the next 20 years emerged. With the series locked at 1-1, it was a do-or-die situation for Lloyd.

And thus, unfolded the first history lesson of the tour. And after India had surged to 178 for one from 65 overs on the first day which ended early due to bad light, Lloyd was staring down the barrel. That's when the bowling tactics changed dramatically on the second day. Michael Holding, playing for the first time at his home ground of Sabina Park and with the crowd egging him on, came around the wicket and targeted the batsmen's bodies rather than their stumps.

'The Battle of Kingston' was the headline in *The Cricketer.* 'Bloodbath at Sabina Park' screamed the headline in *Sportsweek.*

In the 2011 edition of his autobiography *No Holding Back,* Holding admitted: 'We used the drastic tactic of going round the wicket and bowling short. It was out of sheer desperation that we did it. We won, but we upset a lot of people [including Holding's mother!] and it was not far off from Bodyline.'

The carnage began with the second new ball, taken at 199 for one. G.R. Viswanath had the middle finger of his left hand broken, even as he was caught off Holding, who also accounted for both Sunil Gavaskar and Mohinder Amarnath.

Then, at 273 for three, came a heart-stopping moment with opener Aunshuman Gaekwad on a courageous 81. He described the scene to H. Natarajan in the July 2002 issue of *Wisden Asia Cricket* monthly ('Black and blue and red all over'):

> Clive Lloyd...had his bowlers unleash a barrage of short-pitched balls. The intimidation was relentless. I was hit all over the body till I was sore and my fingers swollen. After the umpteenth blow I walked away towards square leg... As I walked back to take strike I gave Mikey (Holding), who was waiting at the top of his run up, the finger. Next ball, I was hit on the left ear. My specs flew off on impact and I bled profusely all over my clothes.

It was a life-threatening injury and Gaekwad admitted that it brought back memories of Indian captain Nari Contractor's brush with death at Bridgetown, Barbados in 1962.

Wrote Holding in his book about his friendship with Gaekwad:

> I wouldn't have blamed Aunshuman for having nothing to do with me following the infamous Jamaica Test of 1976. I hit Aunshuman, who was as gutsy a batsman as there has ever been, with a nasty blow on the ear...and it turned out to be quite a serious injury. It punctured his ear drum and he required an operation. But he never held a grudge and we remain in contact today, sending emails and Christmas cards.

According to Gaekwad, 'There was some doubt over whether I could endure the long flight back home because of the cabin pressure, but I managed. As soon as I got back home, I had to undergo two surgeries because of the damage.'

Brijesh Patel joined the injury list when he was hit in the mouth by Vanburn Holder and went to hospital for stitches. Then came the declaration, with skipper Bedi and B.S. Chandrasekhar, virtual non-batsmen, spared the danger of potential injury and not being able to bowl. Holding had four of the wickets that fell and debutant Wayne Daniel two.

Wrote Suresh Menon in *Bishan: Portrait of a Cricketer*, 'Neither Bedi nor Chandrasekhar were likely to make a difference to the score—they were more desperately needed as bowlers, not batsmen, and Bedi's logic was irrefutable. He declared to protect his bowlers.'

The Ridge that Wasn't

One of the enduring myths is that a ridge suddenly appeared on the pitch on a good length spot on the second day, which caused the ball to fly and endanger the batsmen. This claim was made by Lloyd in his 1980 autobiography *Living for Cricket*.

> I must say I felt a little sorry for them [the Indians] at the time, but there was certainly no deliberate policy on our part to indulge in unfair tactics...In the pitch at the northern end there was a particular spot from which the ball would either fly dangerously or shoot. All the batsmen hit suffered their injuries from this end.

In the book *Fire in Babylon*, inspired by the documentary of the same name by Stevan Riley, author Simon Lister had a rather fanciful theory about this spot: 'The pitch had recently been relaid, and a ridge appeared at the northern end, possibly created by an underground drainage channel.'

However, Holding himself has refuted this 'ridge' theory in both his 1993 autobiography *Whispering Death* and in *No Holding Back* in 2011. In the former, he writes:

> Some people claimed there was a ridge but I never detected one...On that surface, it was inevitable that some batsmen would be hit...especially as we adopted the tactic of bowling from around the wicket. I was not too keen on this method since it gives the batsman little chance of avoiding a bouncer especially against bowlers with plenty of speed, but it was 1-1 in the series and after Australia we were under extreme public pressure to win.

In *No Holding Back*, he writes, 'Many people said the pitch was to blame because there was a ridge, but in truth, we just bowled an awful lot of short balls. Sometimes the ball just took off from a good length on a surface that was full of pace...

Man, it was quick...We went over the top.'

The story of the 'ridge' suddenly appearing out of nowhere on the second day was debunked by *The Times of India*'s famous cricket correspondent K.N. Prabhu in Anandji Dossa's *Cricket Quarterly* (April–June 1976) where he wrote 'the "ridge"...was nothing but a myth.'

In fact, there is a largely unknown story as to how the conspiracy to target the Indian batsmen was hatched the night of the first day's play. And the finger has been pointed at Clyde Walcott, one of the famous 'Three Ws' of Barbados and West Indies cricket. Walcott was chairman of the West Indies selection panel and the brains behind the tactics employed the next day by Lloyd.

This was revealed in 2006 by team treasurer and former Madras Ranji Trophy captain 'Balu' Alaganan to Bhaskeran Thomas, editor of the Tamil Nadu cricket journal, *Straight Bat*. According to Alaganan, it was from commentator and friend Tony Cozier that he learned of the plot. Sadly, both Alaganan and Cozier are no longer with us.

After West Indies reached 391 in their first innings for a lead of 85 runs, came the bizarre turn of events which has led to another myth which is damaging to the image of Indian cricket.

Kunal Pradhan wrote in *Hindustan Times* ('Windies Revival—An Elusive Dream', 16 February 2019), '...Jamaica's Sabina Park, the ground where five Indian batsmen had chosen to be absent hurt rather than face Michael Holding & Co. in 1975 [sic]...'

The players had not 'chosen to be absent hurt', three of them were injured while batting in the first innings, with Gaekwad's the most serious injury. Bedi and Chandrasekhar had injured their hands while attempting to take return catches in West

Indies' first innings. None of them were in any position to bat the second time round. Remember, helmets in Test cricket were still two years away (Chapter 2), and the last straw was Surinder Amarnath, who was not in the playing XI, having to undergo an emergency appendix operation mid-Test.

That the Indian camp resembled the walking wounded was made clear by Dicky Rutnagur in his summing up of the tour for *Wisden Cricketers' Almanack* 1977:

> As, at the end of the tour, the Indian team trudged along the tarmac towards their home-bound aeroplane at Kingston's Norman Manley Airport, they resembled Napoleon's troops on the retreat from Moscow. They were battle-weary and a lot of them were enveloped in plasters and bandages.

The plasters were the campaign ribbons of a controversial and somewhat violent final Test which the West Indies won to prevail 2-1 in a four-Test series.

No Declaration

The story, that Bedi declared the second innings at 97 for 5 in protest, is thus false. The captain himself clarified in Suresh Menon's book that, with five batsmen injured, it was the end of the innings: '...a fact that was later confirmed to me by Bedi who stated that the innings was complete at that stage since there was no one fit to bat. It was *not* [emphasis mine] a declaration.' There may however have been an element of protest around the first innings declaration.

At first, those at the ground thought that Bedi had declared again. But it was only after West Indies had won that a statement was issued by the captain that the Indian innings should be recorded as completed, according to *Wisden*.

Menon also quotes the late Rajan Bala, 'Many years later, Holding admitted to me that he was ashamed of that Test.' However, in his book, among others, Holding makes the claim that Bedi declared the second innings closed 'with only five wickets down'. That left Windies a mere 13 runs to win, which they knocked off in the second over to claim the contentious series 2-1.

The myth of the declaration was dredged up 40 years later in *The Cricketer* (July 2016) which just goes to show how long falsehoods can linger. Ex-Middlesex batsman Paul Smith wrote ('Preparing for Battle'):

> Fear of injury plays heavily on the mind of many tailend batsmen. Such was India captain Bishan Singh Bedi's fear for his batsmen's welfare in Jamaica 1976 that he declared in the fourth [sic] innings when only five wickets were down. He refused to allow his batsmen to face the pace and hostility of the West Indian attack.

My correction was published in the letters section in the September 2016 issue:

> Paul Smith was wrong in stating Bishan Bedi declared in the fourth innings of the 1976 Kingston Test when only five wickets down 'out of fear for his batsmen's welfare'. The scorecard shows there was no declaration—the third innings (not fourth) was closed with five wickets down as five players were injured. The scorecard reads 97 all out with five listed as 'absent hurt'.

On the rest day of the Test, which immediately followed the dramatic second day, manager Polly Umrigar and Bedi called a press conference where Bedi insisted that the game had not been played in the spirit of cricket but had been turned into a 'war'.

The Fire in Babylon documentary shows the Indian team in poor light, with some of the West Indian players making disparaging remarks about the lack of courage of the batsmen. There is also a misleading photo of Gavaskar leading partner Chetan Chauhan off the field in protest in the 1981 Melbourne Test (Chapter 2), with 'India Surrender Match' plastered across it, even as wicketkeeper Deryk Murray intones in the background: 'The Indians thought we were overdoing the fast bowling and surrendered the Test match against the West Indies almost as a show of protest.' It should have been made clear that the footage was not from the Kingston Test. The comments too are misleading, as I can personally attest to.

Remarkably, at a time when cricket telecasts were at a nascent stage in India, Doordarshan sprang a pleasant surprise by showing the highlights of the match. This gave me an opportunity to witness first-hand the intimidatory tactics of the West Indian bowlers and how the Indian batsmen faced up to them.

I was in school in Calcutta at the time and for four days (the match ended one day early) I travelled to the home of famous all-rounder Dattu Phadkar to watch the highlights. This gave me the added advantage of listening to the expert comments of Phadkar, no mean pace bowler himself (Chapter 6).

He was certainly not pleased with Lloyd's tactics as we watched with mounting horror. My two abiding memories are of the Sabina Park crowd baying for blood every time a bouncer was bowled (vividly described by Gavaskar in *Sunny Days*) and debutant Daniel innocently looking at his hand as if the ball had slipped after he had delivered a beamer.

The two umpires were mute spectators when they should

have stepped in to warn the bowlers, but they feared for their lives from the local mobs and stayed mum. Even the doyen of West Indian cricket writers, the late Tony Cozier, expressed his dissatisfaction over their inaction.

It took many years and was surely not the sole reason, but the bumper barrage at Sabina Park and the umpires failing in their duties eventually led, through a series of other events, to the ICC (International Cricket Council) imposing a restriction on bouncers, and appointing Match Referees and neutral umpires for all international matches.

So something good came of that Test match after all, for which Bedi deserves credit, instead of the approbation he has received in some quarters.

9

....

PACE LIKE FIRE

Still I hear the conk of the ball on his head.

—David Murray

17 March 1962 was one of the darkest days in the history of Indian sport. On this day, India's cricket captain, Nariman 'Nari' Jamshedji Contractor was struck on the head by the infamous fast bowler Charlie Griffith in the match against Barbados at Kensington Oval, Bridgetown, and the world held its breath in collective agony as he hovered between life and death for five excruciating days.

Contractor was 28 at the time, and was halfway through the tour of West Indies, which a demoralized and devastated Indian team would eventually lose 5-0. That Contractor is still with us, well into his 80s, means that the cricket gods must have smiled on him: as he told me in an interview for BBC on the 40th anniversary of the incident in 2002[13], the 'concussion of the brain' that he suffered was, back then, considered 99 per cent fatal.

It is no wonder that the first thought that struck Aunshuman Gaekwad, when he was hit by Holding at Sabina Park 14 years later, was the Contractor incident. It took years for the trauma to heal, even though Contractor made a full and miraculous recovery, largely due to the round-the-clock care by manager and former captain Ghulam Ahmed, one of the finest gentlemen Indian cricket has produced.

So, what are the myths surrounding this near-tragedy? Quite simply, they centre around the kind of delivery that Griffith delivered that fateful day and how Contractor dealt with it.

Most West Indians have, over the years, tried to explain it away as the batsman ducking under what he thought was a bouncer but which was not. The only available photo of the incident indeed shows Contractor squatting, almost on his haunches, supported by his bat, with wicketkeeper David Allan, bowler Griffith and the two slips looking on, concerned. In *My Autobigraphy*, Garry Sobers states:

> ...Nari Contractor was hit while playing for India against Barbados when he ducked into a ball that didn't get up from Charlie Griffith. Charlie was going to appeal for leg before wicket but I stopped him as I could see that Contractor was in serious trouble and, in fact, nearly died.

However, in the book *Fire In Babylon*, it is written: 'He [wicketkeeper David Murray] ...had seen Nari Contractor hit by that infamous Charlie Griffith *bouncer* [emphasis mine] in

---

[13]Gulu Ezekiel, '40 years after Bridgetown', accessed at: http://news.bbc.co.uk/sport2/hi/cricket/1876840.stm

1962. "Just a schoolboy, but still I hear the *conk* of the ball on his head." Murray, born in 1950, played 19 Tests and 10 ODIs for West Indies from 1973 to 1982.

It appears that the Barbados players decided to stick to the line that the Griffith delivery was harmless and that Contractor ducked into and thus the bowler was not to blame. This is strongly refuted by Mansur Ali Khan Pataudi, who was vice captain to Contractor on the tour, till he was thrust into the captaincy, following the incident. In his 1969 autobiography *Tiger's Tale*, he wrote:

...Nari Contractor received a ball from Griffith which was short of a length, and it rose very abruptly. Nari had no time to play any sort of shot, but at the last moment hunched his shoulders. Even from the distance of the dressing room, we could hear the sickening thud as the ball struck his head.

It was a delivery which has since been the subject of much discussion. One suggestion is that the ball did not, in fact, rise above stump height. As an eye witness from reasonably close range, I can dismiss this as completely inaccurate.

Contractor is about five feet nine in height, and when hit was clearly standing upright without having attempted any stroke. In fact, he did not move a muscle until the very last second when he appeared to pick up the ball for the first time, then he hunched into his right shoulder in a protective gesture.

It should also be remembered that Contractor was an already extremely competent and experienced Test batsman, not easily deceived, and still less likely to be scared, by the very best fast bowling.

Pataudi also refers to umpire Hugh B. de Cortez Jordan at square leg sensationally calling Griffith for throwing in the second innings as '[displaying] his own brand of courage...It confirmed our opinion that at times during this match, Charlie's action did not accord with the definition of a fair delivery stated in the book of laws.'

It was courageous indeed on the part of Jordan, who was a local, and he enraged the large crowd that was baying for Indian blood with his call. This is what Contractor told me in the 2002 interview:

> In those days, there was no sightscreen at the pavilion end from where he was bowling and the wicket was in line with the dressing rooms. As he started to run in for the fourth ball, somebody suddenly opened a window in the pavilion. The thought flashed in my mind that I would play this delivery and then tell them to close it. In retrospect, I now realize I was not concentrating 100 per cent and that was the reason I was hit. I turned my head a fraction but it hit me at a 90-degree angle and I fell on my knees. Photos show me sitting down and it was said at the time that I had ducked into the ball. That is not correct. The photo was taken after I had sunk to my knees, still clutching the bat. It was a short-pitched delivery, or a bouncer.

Rutnagur, the Indian-born journalist who would later immigrate to England and who was editor of the short-lived *The Indian Cricket Field Annual*, covered the tour for *Wisden Cricketers' Almanack* and wrote this in the 1963 edition:

> What most of the outside world heard about the incident was that Contractor was struck through ducking to a ball delivered by Charlie Griffith which never rose beyond the

height of the stumps.

Contractor did not duck into the ball. He got behind it to play at it—he probably wanted to fend it away towards short-leg—but could not judge the height to which it would fly, bent back from the waist in a desperate, split-second attempt to avoid it and was just above the right ear.

Rutnagur wrote much the same about the fateful delivery in his report for the 1962-63 edition of *The Indian Cricket Field Annual*. In the editorial section, he made it amply clear that he considered Griffith a chucker, something Contractor himself all these years has refused to say.

However, in an interview with Clayton Murzello in *Backspin* magazine ('On the Spot with Nari Contractor', autumn 2014) he said in reply to the question: 'Was Charlie Griffith a chucker?'

I have never said he was a chucker, never have, never will, but when he came to India in 1966-67 and when I saw him bowl, he was not the Charlie Griffith who bowled to me in 1962. In 1962, he ran in differently to what he did in 1966-67. His action had changed completely. It is for people to decide. K.N. Prabhu was there covering the series and he felt Griffith chucked. Our boys felt he chucked—Vijay Manjrekar, Polly Umrigar—everybody felt the same.

When I asked him the same question in my 2002 interview, Contractor replied, 'I can't say for sure, as when I was batting, I never had a side view of his action.'

Writing in *Sportsweek*'s Flashback series,[14] journalist Berry Sarbadhikary, who was reporting on the match, described the 'bouncer' and the manner in which Contractor attempted to evade it, in much the same manner as Rutnagur did for *Wisden*.

---

[14]'When Contractor Hovered Between Life and Death', *Sportsweek*, 8 July 1973

Rutnagur, in his editorial, made an ominous prediction about Griffith being included in the team to England in 1963. West Indies captain Frank Worrell, on the eve of the 1962 match, had warned the Indians at a party about Griffith's action, and after the incident swore that he would never choose him in any side he led. At that stage, Griffith had played just one Test in 1960, so his selection came as a shock. Rutnagur wrote: 'I have now grave misgivings about the tour [England 1963] being a happy one...I wonder whether the world is in store for what could be a most entertaining series or another of those bitter cricketing feuds.'

In fact, Griffith had an outstanding series with 32 wickets in five Tests, being chosen as one of *Wisden's* Five Cricketers of the Year. But it was not long before respected cricketers such as Richie Benaud, Ted Dexter, Ken Barrington and Bobby Simpson publicly called out his action. Apart from the 1962 match, he was also called for throwing in a tour match in England in 1966.

It was a stigma Griffith carried with him throughout his career and which he strenuously denied in his 1970 autobiography *Chucked Around*. In it, he makes the false claim that Contractor must have been wary of facing his bouncer after he had hit Vijay Manjrekar on the nose. In fact, Manjrekar was hit *after* Contractor, who was stuck in the third over of the Indian innings, and followed his captain to hospital for an X-ray. Griffith also states that Manjrekar was out soon after when, in fact, he retired hurt on two, immediately after being hit—and scored a gallant unbeaten 100 in the second innings, following treatment.

> I bowled him a ball just short of a good length and rising about bail height. He seemed to have seen it and was

shaping to play it. Then, suddenly, he ducked. Poor fellow, he was struck on the ball of the head. The blow resounded all around the ground.

The controversy over Contractor's injury and then being called for chucking in the same match, obviously left Griffith a shattered man and he claims in his book that he felt like quitting the game. He attacks both Worrell and umpire Jordan, asking why the no-ball chucking call was not made *before* (Griffith's emphasis) he struck Contractor—which is odd, since it happened on just the fifth ball of the third over and his second of the innings. There are many such contradictions in the book, in which he spends five pages taunting the Indians' fear of pace, attacking some individuals and largely feeling sorry for himself.

Rutnagur, in the editorial of his annual, wrote:

> When a pace bowler delivers with a crooked elbow and its corollary, a jerk, the bouncer is not related to the length of the ball and trajectory. Except the readers of two or three Indian newspapers who had their correspondents on the spot [including Prabhu of *Times of India*], the rest of the world read the description of biased and unknowledgeable agency reporters, who wrote that Contractor 'ducked' into a short ball that did not rise. Nothing could be further from the truth.

So just how quick was Griffith? These are the words of Trinidad and West Indies batsman Charlie Davis (Chapter 2): 'He was the most lethal man who ever bowled a cricket ball.'[15]

Indeed, courage was in Contractor's DNA. In 1959, in the second Test at Lord's, he had two ribs broken by Brian Statham, an injury that made it difficult for him to even breathe. Yet, he

---

[15]*Sportsworld*, 21-27 June 1989

battled on to 81 and 11 not out in the second innings.

In 1962, after a series of life-saving brain operations in Bridgetown and another in Vellore, Tamil Nadu, where he had a metal plate inserted in his skull, it was through courage of the highest order that by October 1963—18 months after the near-fatal incident—he was back doing what he loved best, playing cricket, though never again Test cricket. This, when a year earlier, he had been half blind and barely able to walk a few steps. And, in the semifinal of the Duleep Trophy at Bombay in December, came the first century on his comeback, 144 for West Zone versus East Zone.

Contractor kept up his consistent batting and was in contention for a place in the Indian team for the twin tours to Australia and New Zealand in 1967–68. This is where the BCCI stepped in out of concern for Contractor's welfare. They dispatched Ghulam Ahmed to speak to Nari and his wife Dolly. This was a man whom Nari had always maintained was his saviour and when Ahmed requested them to drop the plans for a Test comeback, both husband wife agreed, albeit reluctantly. The retirement from all cricket came in 1970–71.

The man who marked his first-class debut for Gujarat with a century in each innings (152 and 102 not out) against Baroda in November 1952 at Baroda, thereby emulating Australia's Arthur Morris, ended it with scores of 20 and 53 not out, again for Gujarat versus Baroda at Ahmedabad on 12 to 14 December 1970.

His first-class record, before and after the injury, makes for interesting reading.

Till injury: M: 94; I: 159; NO: 9; R: 6,076; Av: 40.50; 100s: 17; 50s: 27.

After injury: 44; 75; 9; 2,535; 38.40; 100s: 5; 50s:13.

Like Frank Sinatra's iconic song 'My Way', and its lyrics 'Regrets I have a few, but then again, too few to mention,'

Contractor has lived with just one regret these last nearly 60 years—'not getting to play for my country again after my head injury in Barbados', as he told Murzello for *Backspin* in 2014. But a grateful nation never forgot.

The Fear Factor

Till the arrival of Sunil Manohar Gavaskar on the scene in 1971 (see Chapter 2), all the main Test batting records for India were held by Pahlanji 'Polly' Ratanji Umrigar—most Tests (59), most runs (3,631), most centuries (12) and 35 wickets as well.

But just as Charlie Griffith lived his entire life with the stigma of being called a chucker, Umrigar had to bear the label of being scared of fast bowling, because of just one series (in England 1952) and against one bowler, 'fiery' Fred Trueman.

This, despite excelling on two tours to West Indies, in 1953 and 1962. On the first tour of the Caribbean by an Indian team, Umrigar was the outstanding batsman with 560 runs at 62.22, including two centuries and four fifties.

India did well to lose just one out of five Tests on that tour, but when they returned nine years later, they suffered a 5-0 whitewash. Umrigar stood out amongst the ruins, with 445 runs at 49.44, including one century and three fifties, far above Bapu Nadkarni in second place with 33.71.

In 1953, Umrigar's centuries came in the first Test at Port of Spain, Trinidad and the fifth at Kingston, Jamaica with fast bowler Frank King leading the home bowling attack.

In 1962, in what would be his final series, his 172 not out in the fourth Test at Port of Spain was India's highest in the series and one of only two centuries. It was a memorable match for him, even though India were beaten by seven wickets. In West Indies' first innings, he returned figures of 5 for 107, making him only the second Indian after Vinoo Mankad to achieve this 'double' in a Test match.

This time, West Indies had in their ranks the formidable Wesley Hall, one of the all-time great fast bowlers, as well as Charlie Stayers and Garry Sobers, who was pretty nippy when bowling pace.

Umrigar also stood up unflinchingly to the thunderbolts hurled by Hall and Roy Gilchrist in the 1958–59 home series. Gilchrist, aka 'the wild man of cricket', was not only one of the fastest of all time but also the most dangerous, making liberal use of the bouncer and beamer during his short and stormy international career. He targeted the batsman's body more than the stumps and grabbed 26 wickets in four Tests at 16.11, striking terror in the hearts of the Indian batsmen. Umrigar's creditable average of 42.12 included three fifties.

His stats against West Indies are pretty impressive—16 Tests, 1,372 runs, 50.81 average, 100s: 3; 50s: 10, HS: 172 not out.

That should have buried the myth of his fear of fast bowling for all time, yet Umrigar's name will always be linked to Trueman and that disastrous tour of 1952, in which India was well beaten in the first three Tests and only escaped with a draw in the fourth and final, due to rain.

England's Greatest?

It was 1952, Trueman's maiden Test series, and he would end his career as arguably England's greatest fast bowler and one of the fastest too.

The opening Test at Trueman's home ground at Headingley, Leeds saw Umrigar become the Yorkshireman's first wicket in the first innings, as India reached a respectable 293 all out. England replied with 334 and the match was evenly poised as

India began their second innings.

What unfolded next was Indian cricket's ultimate batting humiliation, at least till Lord's in 1974, when they were skittled out for 42.

In an unprecedented start to an innings, India lost their first four wickets without a run on the board, with Trueman grabbing three of them and Alec Bedser one. Pankaj Roy, Datta Gaekwad, Madhav Mantri and first innings centurion Vijay Manjrekar all fell without opening their accounts, and the crowd was in an uproar as the giant scoreboard showed 0 for 4 in the space of just 14 balls.

As Manjrekar was bowled by Trueman, captain Len Hutton pointed to the scoreboard. 'Take a good look at it,' he urged his players. 'You'll never see another like it in a Test.'[16]

Trueman was now on a hat-trick, that too on debut; however, he just missed captain Vijay Hazare's off stump by a whisker. India limped their way to 165 but the damage to their psyche was profound and they never recovered.

In the Trueman book, Gaekwad recalled the mood of the Indians:

> We were shell-shocked. There is no other word for it. To be naught for four in a Test match was incredibly upsetting. We'd been very much in the game until then, but Freddie changed all that. He was focusing totally on out-and-out speed. He didn't have the control of later years but it did not matter. As the wickets went down, he was shouting and swearing because that's how he thought a fast bowler should be. He was making all kinds of elaborate gestures and loving every minute.

---

[16]Chris Waters, *Fred Trueman: The Authorised Biography*, Aurum, 2011

Umrigar had a miserable series with scores of 8, 9, 5, 14, 4, 3 and 0: 43 runs at 6.14, falling to Trueman four times.

Interviewed for Anandji Dossa's *Cricket Quarterly* in January 1975, Hutton expressed surprise at the manner in which the Indian batsmen capitulated to Trueman:

> I was very much surprised in 1952 to see the way that some of your batsmen played Trueman, who I don't think was all that fast then. Admittedly, he bowled a few short balls and that sort of thing, but I am surprised they didn't play him better than they did. I wonder if they had a great fear of being hit. I wonder if this was predominant in their minds and they gave me the impression that they were a little scared of Trueman.

Following the Leeds trauma, more disaster was to follow in the next Test at Old Trafford. India became the first team in Test history to be dismissed twice in the same day—58 and 82, with Trueman in the first innings leading the rout with 8 for 31. They would remain his career best figures.

All the Indian batsmen suffered under the onslaught, but the stigma stayed with Umrigar alone. To the best of my knowledge, there is no footage or still photos to corroborate it, at least not any that I have come across. The reports in the 1953 edition of *Wisden* or in *The Cricketer* also do not specifically mention Umrigar retreating to square leg in the face of Trueman's hostility, but there is no doubt that he was visibly intimidated by Trueman's thunderbolts.

Hemu Adhikari was also one among the many flops in the series. He was manager of the Indian team on tours to England in 1971 and 1974, and during one of the tours, Trueman on meeting him is said to have quipped, 'Ah Colonel, I see you have got your colour back,' indicating that he went pale with fear when facing his bowling in 1952.

Writing in *The Sunday Times of India* ('Cricket is poetry in motion', 17 March 1996), Nick Bridge, who was then posted in New Delhi as New Zealand's High Commissioner, recalls his first cricket memory as an eight-year-old—of Umrigar hitting four sixes. It was in the match against Hampshire at Bournemouth, in an innings of 165 not out, after the Test series had ended and the sun was shining, something very rare at that ground. Bridge writes:

> I remember thinking at the time that it was dreadfully unfair for Indians to have to play in such freezing, miserable conditions. On reflection, the conditions in the Tests in England that year were such that it could be said that India was really the first team to play day/ night cricket—without lights.

Some of the stories narrated about Umrigar appear fanciful and exaggerated. Indian and Pakistani batsmen were the butt of jokes back then, for their weakness against fast bowling, and cruel jokes and harsh comments were often directed at them.

Famed umpire Dickie Bird's *My Autobiography* is reportedly the highest selling cricket autobiography of all time; Bird is a known spinner of colourful cricket yarns and the book is full of them. One such tale concerns the Indians' tour match against Yorkshire at Bramall Lane in 1959, where Bird was 12th man. Bird claims that Umrigar was playing a kind of game of hide-and-seek over Trueman's availability or not for the match, as he was under treatment for an injury, and ultimately Trueman played, at which Umrigar opted out.

In fact, neither of them played in the match that Bird refers to. Bird also refers to Umrigar as the captain of the touring side, when Datta Gaekwad was the captain. Bird says that Umrigar was one of the finest players against spin and medium pace, but 'decidedly ill at ease when faced with anything quicker'.

Yet, less than two weeks later, Umrigar scored 118 in the third Test at Old Trafford against the bowling of Trueman and Harold Rhodes, who was considered to be the fastest bowler in England at the time. And his exemplary record against West Indies proves that he was no slouch against their fast bowlers either.

In an interview to Bhaskeran Thomas for the Tamil Nadu cricket journal *Straight Bat*, Umrigar offered a somewhat implausible theory for his batting in the 1952 series:

> When queried about these 'exaggerated accounts', Umrigar explained that he never evaded a fast bowler. In England in those days, wickets were uncovered and after each deluge it was difficult to distinguish the playing strip from the green outfield. Plus, the bowlers' boot marks were like cattle footholds. This encouraged Truman and Bedser to pitch the ball on these dangerous marks, to scare the wits out of the Indian batsmen. He explicitly stated how he had to come a bit away from the leg stump in order to hit the ball over extra cover. Unfortunately, he either dragged the ball on to the stumps or nudged a catch into the slip fielders' hands. And that was the reason why his stumps were rearranged, he said.

Incidentally, Mohammed Azharuddin used the same reasoning after the 1989 tour of West Indies, where he and others in the team were accused of backing away from fast bowling. Azharuddin reasoned that it was to make space on the offside and quoted Don Bradman's example in the 1932–33 Bodyline series to Suresh Menon, journalist and editor of the erstwhile *Wisden India*.

Outside the Test series, Umrigar had an outstanding tour with 1,688 runs and three double centuries. In addition, there was a century in the Old Trafford Test in 1959 as well.

While Indian batsmen have often succumbed to fast bowling, the theory that they play spin well is not borne out by the facts. Right from the first tour to India, by England in 1933–34 in which left-arm spin master Hedley Verity was the leading wicket-taker, Indian batsmen have both at home and abroad shown their frailty to the likes of Lance Gibbs (West Indies), Derek Underwood (England), Australia's Ashley Mallet and Nathan Lyon, and Muttiah Muralitharan of Sri Lanka.

Australian leg-spin legend Shane Warne has been a notable failure against India both in Tests and ODIs, but unheralded spin bowlers like Paul Harris (South Africa), Ray Price (Zimbabwe), Shaun Udal (England) and Michael Clarke (Australia) have also troubled Indian batsmen over the years.

Coming back to Umrigar, few Indian cricketers have served the game so nobly and selflessly in so many capacities after their playing days, both with the BCCI and Mumbai Cricket Association (MCA). Manager of teams to New Zealand and West Indies in 1975–76 and to Australia in 1977–78, captain Bishan Singh Bedi told me that Umrigar was 'a giant of a man in every sense of the word'.

Umrigar, who passed away in 2006 at the age of 80, was known to one and all as Polly kaka (paternal uncle in Marathi). In an affectionate tribute to him in *Mid-Day*[17], Clayton Murzello lauded his administrative achievements, including the major role he played in building the Wankhede Stadium in 1974: 'Cricket was Umrigar's oxygen. Indian cricket can never have a servant like him.'

---

[17]Clayton Murzello, 'All-rounder On and Off the Field', *Mid-Day*, 25 April 2019

10

INDIAN CRICKET'S 'GRAND SLAM' MOMENT

Indian cricket did not begin in 1971.
—*G.S. Ramchand*

It was in 1968, in New Zealand under the captaincy of 'Tiger' Pataudi, that India won a series on foreign soil for the first time. The next time that happened was in 1971, an epochal year for Indian cricket, with victories for the first time in West Indies and England. In that period (1968–71), India played just two series at home, drawing 1-1 with New Zealand and losing 3-1 to Australia. There were no foreign tours in between, at a time when the Indian Test team's calendar was sketchy at best.

At a cricket function in Mumbai some years back, G.S. Ramchand was miffed at all the attention being lavished on the heroes of 1971 under the captaincy of Ajit Wadekar. This led to his comment that Indian cricket did not begin in 1971.

Ramchand was India's captain when India defeated Australia, led by Richie Benaud for the first time in December 1959. Kanpur was the venue and off spinner Jasu Patel the hero, with 14 wickets in the match. India, however, lost the five-Test series 2-1.

In November 2019, at the end of the second Test at Kolkata against Bangladesh—the first day/night Test on Indian soil—captain Virat Kohli, perhaps overwhelmed at the historic occasion and in the backyard of BCCI president Sourav Ganguly, made a statement that irked Sunil Gavaskar. Kohli, after wrapping up the series 2-0, commented that the Indian team 'learned to stand up and give it back. It all started with Dada's [Ganguly] team and we are just carrying it forward.'

That led to a short, sharp history lesson from Gavaskar, who pointed out during his TV stint at the end of the match, in an echo of Ramchand's words:

> A lot of people still think that Indian cricket started only in the 2000s. But the Indian team won overseas in the '70s. The Indian team also won away in 1986. India also drew series overseas. They lost like other teams did.
>
> The Indian captain [Kohli] said that this thing started in 2000 with Dada's team. I know Dada is the BCCI president, so maybe Kohli wanted to say nice things about him. But India were also winning in the '70s and '80s. He wasn't born then.

Gavaskar should know. He is the only player who was a part of the Indian team through all its glorious moments in the 1970s and 80s. His debut series in West Indies in 1971 was a sensational one (Chapter 2), with a world record tally (774 runs) for a debutant that still stands. Then came victory over the top cricketing nation at the time, at the Oval in 1971.

In 1976 at Port of Spain, Trinidad (Chapter 8) came the world record run chase steered by his own century and that of G.R. Viswanath. India won a Test match in Australia (albeit against a third-string side) for the first time in 1977–78, though they lost the series 3-2 and in 1979 at the Oval, Gavaskar's sensational 221 took India to the doorstep of a historic victory.

The 1981 win in the third Test at Melbourne (Chapter 2) under his captaincy saw India square the series 1-1 against a full-strength Australian team, and in 1986 he was part of the team that beat England 2-0 on their soil for only the second time since 1971. The 1985–86 series in Australia was also drawn (0-0), both these with Kapil Dev leading.

But, that was not all. Between 1983 and 1985, India seemingly out of nowhere dominated the world of one-day cricket, beginning with the stunning victory in the third Prudential World Cup in England in 1983 (Chapter 7).

Victorious Swansong

Gavaskar's swansong as captain was marked by an emphatic victory in the Benson & Hedges World Championship of Cricket (WCC) in February–March 1985, staged to mark the 150th anniversary of the state of Victoria. It was a one-off event, featuring all seven Test-playing nations, a sort of mini-World Cup and India remained undefeated through the tournament.

Before that came the Rothmans Asia Cup at Sharjah in April 1984, and just after the WCC was the Rothmans four-nation tournament (India, Australia, Pakistan and England), also in Sharjah in 1985, featuring one of the all-time great comebacks in one-day cricket history.

It was cricket's equivalent of tennis' Grand Slam and, remarkably, all these victories came abroad. (In sporting parlance, the Grand Slam pertains to a tennis player winning all four Majors in the same calendar year—Wimbledon (UK), the French, US and Australian Opens). At home in that same period, 1983 to 1985, conversely India were beaten by West Indies (5-0 in 1983–84), Australia (3-0 with two no-results in 1984–85) and England (4-1 in 1984–85)—apart from losing the Test series to West Indies and England, thus turning on its head all the theories about being tigers at home and kittens abroad.

The only ODI series victory at home in that period came in 1983–84, with India winning both its matches against Pakistan, hot on the heels of the Prudential World Cup stunner.

This is not to downplay India's record under Ganguly's captaincy from 2000 to 2005; international cricket had become cut-throat, epitomized by the take-no-prisoners style of the all-conquering Australians under Steve Waugh. Ganguly gave the Aussies, with their infamous 'mental disintegration' tactics, back in their own coin. Vitally, he also helped restore faith among Indian cricket fans in the aftermath of the match-fixing scandal which blew up in 2000.

At home came one of the great Test comebacks of all time, bouncing back from a trouncing in the first Test at Mumbai at the hands of Australia, to stage tremendous fightbacks at Kolkata and Chennai, to win 2-1. Then in Waugh's last series in 2003–04, India came within a whisker of a first series win in Australia, before drawing 1-1. There was also a drawn series in England in 2002 and, in 2004, India for the first time won both a Test and ODI series in Pakistan. Here, it must be noted that an injured Ganguly led in only the third and final Test at Rawalpindi, which India won to take the series 2-1. His deputy Rahul Dravid led in the first at Multan, won by an innings by India and in the second at Lahore, which India lost.

Dravid, in fact, had notable series victories in England in

2007 (the first since 1986) and West Indies in 2006 (the first since 1971), where India had been beaten 2-1 under Ganguly's captaincy in 2002.

The myth that India began winning Tests abroad only under Ganguly's captaincy is perhaps due to his record of 11 wins against 10 defeats. However, these figures are misleading. Of these 11, only two (one each in England and Australia) came in the so-called SENA (South Africa, England, New Zealand and Australia) nations, the rest in Sri Lanka, Zimbabwe, Bangladesh and West Indies. Apart from the Pakistan case, the only series won abroad by India during Ganguly's captaincy stint from 2000 to 2005—against defeats in South Africa, New Zealand and West Indies—were two-Test series in Bangladesh and Zimbabwe, hardly an impressive record.

If one goes by white-ball cricket, the first round exit in the 2007 ICC World Cup in West Indies will always be a black mark for Dravid. Ganguly's biggest achievements in this regard was becoming only the second Indian captain to lead India to the final of a World Cup (South Africa 2003) and also the final of the 2000 ICC knockout tournament (now Champions Trophy). Both were lost, the former to Australia and the latter to New Zealand, while in the 2002 Champions Trophy in Sri Lanka, the final against the hosts was twice disrupted by rain and India shared the title. But winning the NatWest tri-series final against England at Lord's in 2002 (Sri Lanka being the third participant), remains an iconic moment in Indian cricket.

Just as Pataudi built a formidable spin bowling attack and raised India's fielding levels, only for Wadekar to take over the reins and become the first Indian captain to win three Test series on the trot (1971 to 1973), so Dravid also built on Ganguly's leadership skills in encouraging and supporting youngsters like Harbhajan Singh, Zaheer Khan and Virender Sehwag.

Every Indian captain, from C.K. Nayudu to Lala Amarnath, Vijay Hazare to Ramchand, Pataudi to Wadekar, Gavaskar to Kapil Dev, right down to Ganguly, Dravid, Mahendra Singh Dhoni and the present incumbent, Virat Kohli, has left their unique imprint on Indian cricket while the team has gone through ups and downs.

Though countless words have been written on India's maiden triumph in the World Cup under the inspiring captaincy of Kapil, the current generation—captain Kohli included—need to be reminded about that golden period of one-day domination (1983–85), aka the Grand Slam.

So, where did this term originate? It was used as a headline in the Madras edition of *The Indian Express* (where I worked from 1982–91) after India won the Rothmans four-nation tournament in Sharjah in March 1985, just weeks after the WCC triumph, to round off the golden run.

'Yes, it's Grand Slam', was the headline in the daily the day after the final against Australia. So imagine our surprise a week later, when our cross-town rival *The Hindu*'s sports magazine *Sportstar* (13 April 1985) carried as its cover story headline: 'Yes, it's a Grand Slam'!

The Grand Slam busted enough myths to fill a book. In fact, a booklet was produced, marking the occasion, called *Wills Tribute to Excellence: Champions of One-Day Cricket*,[18] with contributions by cricketers and journalists from around the world, and numerous photographs and statistics.

As England's famed cricket writer Scyld Berry noted in his article 'Keeping Their Heads': 'Had Kapil not been inspired to play the innings of his life, 175 not out, against Zimbabwe

---

[18]Khalid Ansari (editor), *Wills Book of Cricket: Champions of One-Day Cricket*, Orient Longman, 1985

at Tunbridge Wells, this book might never have come to be written.'

Before the 1983 Prudential World Cup, such a publication would not even have figured in the wildest dreams of the most die-hard Indian cricket fan who, like our cricketers themselves, did not take the limited-overs version of cricket seriously.

Test cricket was still king in India and the BCCI staged just one one-day series at home in 1981–82, India beating the touring Englishmen 2-1. This was a good 10 years after the inaugural one-day international, an impromptu game held at the MCG in January 1971, to give the spectators some compensation for a washed-out Test match.

The Board's reluctance to embrace the 50-over game (60 overs in England till 1983), was echoed in 2007 when they were dragged kicking and screaming into the inaugural ICC T20 World Cup in South Africa in 2007. At the time, Indian board officials swore at the newfangled 20/20 concept; now they swear by it.

Victory in England in 1983, and then in South Africa in 2007, was an eye-opener for those same officials. The former saw an explosion of ODIs around the world and particularly in Asia, and in 2008 the introduction of the Indian Premier League changed the face of cricket forever—for better or for worse.

No-hopers to world champs

What prompted Australia's captain Kim Hughes at the 1983 Prudential World Cup to pick out India as the 'dark horses' for the title, before the championships began, remains a mystery. For nobody in India would have dared to make such a prediction. Even the Indian sports magazines did not stick out their necks in their World Cup preview issues.

Sportstar in its World Cup special dated 4 June 1983, captioned a photo of Kapil Dev thus: 'If India can spring a surprise or two in the World Cup, it is more likely than not that its skipper would come up with an ace.' Really, that was all Indian fans could realistically hope for.

English critics were even harsher. *The Cricketer* (June 1983) did not even bother to mention India in their curtain-raiser, while founder/editor of *Wisden Cricket Monthly* (June 1983), David Frith was scathing in his assessment of India's chances. Even the staunchest of Indian supporters would have found it hard to disagree with him, such was India's dire record in the previous two editions of the Prudential World Cup in 1975 and 1979. Most previews picked Pakistan as the team to beat West Indies. There were, however, murmurs that the champions were more vulnerable this time around, due to their ageing players and the defections of the 'rebels' to South Africa earlier that year.

India had played their first ODIs in England on the disastrous 1974 tour, losing both. In the run-up to the Prudential World Cup, their record was disappointing: Played: 40; Won: 12; Lost: 28.

Months later, still smarting from their shock defeat in the final at Lord's on 25 June, West Indies under Clive Lloyd came to India with a mission. A distraught Lloyd had announced his retirement from cricket in the shocked West Indies dressing room after the Lord's humiliation, only to withdraw it the next day under pressure from teammates and board officials.

That West Indies won the five-Test series 3-0 and made a 5-0 clean sweep of the ODI series in India may have come as a modicum of solace to the twice champions, but nothing could take away the glory from the holders of the World Cup.

A few months later in April 1984, Sharjah staged the

inaugural Rothmans Asia Cup with India, Pakistan and Sri Lanka as the three teams in the round-robin event.

Just 10 months earlier, in the triumphant Indian dressing room at Lord's, England's famous wicketkeeper Godfrey Evans had presented Syed Kirmani with the Gordon's Dry Gin Trophy for best wicketkeeper in the Prudential World Cup. The giant bottle that came with it though was wasted on the teetotaler Kiri.

Now, Kirmani found himself making way in the playing XI for Delhi's wicketkeeper/batsman Surinder Khanna, who had last donned national colours in the second Prudential World Cup in England in 1979.

With Gavaskar continuing his recent trend of batting lower down the order, the new opening pair was Khanna and Ghulam Parkar. It was left to genial manager Abbas Ali Baig to break the news to Kirmani, that he was being replaced by the reserve wicketkeeper-cum-opener, for the sake of team balance.

Once Lanka had stunned Pakistan in the opening game and India then crushed the Lankans by 10 wickets, the match between India and Pakistan was a mere formality. Batting first, by lunch and with two wickets down, the Indians knew that they would win the title on run quotient even if they lost the match.

Khanna top scored with 51 not out in the first match and once again set the tempo with 56 as India romped home by 54 runs. Two Man of the Match awards meant that Khanna was also Man of the Series. India, with four points from two matches, were the first Asia Cup winners.

The run up to the World Championship of Cricket, which began at the MCG on 17 February 1985 with England taking on the hosts, could not have been worse for the Indian nation, in light of which the travails of the national cricket team pale into insignificance.

David Gower's English team landed in India on the very day of the assassination of Prime Minister Indira Gandhi (31 October 1984), and hot-footed it to Sri Lanka to get some much needed practice, with the country in turmoil.

When they returned, they were trounced in the opening Test at Bombay, with teenage leg spin sensation L. Sivaramakrishnan taking six wickets in both innings in a sensational performance. He took six wickets in the first innings of the next Test at New Delhi as well, but things went pear-shaped after that, both for the teenager as well as his team.

India crashed to defeat by eight wickets and the casualty was Kapil Dev, who was dropped for the next Test at Calcutta (which was drawn amidst shocking crowd scenes), after playing a rash stroke in the second innings. It was also the last Test in the career of Sandeep Patil.

Kapil was back for the fourth Test at Madras, but the fight had seemingly gone out of the Indian camp, and they succumbed by nine wickets to lose the series 2-1, even though it had begun so promisingly, with the fifth and final test at Kanpur drawn. One silver lining was the emergence of the new batting sensation Mohammed Azharuddin, with three centuries in his first three Tests—still a unique record.

The ODI series went no better, India beaten 4-1, though Ravi Shastri was somewhat surprisingly chosen Man of the Series, in a sign of things to come. Though there were signs that he would be named as the new captain, in the end Gavaskar retained the captaincy, but the whole cloak-and-dagger manner of it made him decide that he would relinquish the post at the end of the Australian tournament. The revolving door captaincy game between him and Kapil thus came to a merciful end.

In 22-year-old Sadanand Viswanath from Karnataka, India were fielding their third wicketkeeper in three tournaments abroad, following Kirmani and Khanna. What raised eyebrows however was the inclusion of Sivaramakrishnan (Siva for short), for India already had one spinner in Shastri and surely spinners had no place in one-day games?

That was certainly the perceived wisdom and in the three World Cups (1975, 1979 and 1983), the only spin bowling feat of note was England off spinner Vic Mark's 5-39 versus Sri Lanka at Taunton in the 1983 edition.

It was India's medium pacers who had excelled in the victorious campaign. The only exception was Shastri with 3-26 in the opening shock win against West Indies at Old Trafford, as he polished off the pesky Windies tail. But in the WCC, Shastri's main role would be as opening partner for the irrepressible K. Srikkanth.

Winning with Spin

The WCC would put to rest once and for all the myth of spinners having little or no role in ODIs and it was captain Gavaskar who saw to this with his expert handling of the bowlers.

West Indies was blazing a trail in Australia ever since the advent of Kerry Packer's World Series Cricket, which ran for two seasons (1977–78 and 1978–79). They were frequent visitors Down Under after that as well, and had totally dominated both the Test matches against Australia as well as the World Series Cup one-day tri-series. In fact, they had just retained their World Series Cup title, beating Australia 2-1 in the finals, with Sri Lanka being the third team in the fray. This was their fourth title, having earlier clinched the cup in 1979–80, 1981–82 and 1983–84.

They were thus hot favourites for the WCC title as well,

and were placed in Group B with New Zealand and Sri Lanka. Group A consisted of India, Pakistan, England and Australia. In his preview piece for the official souvenir, Dilip Vengsarkar hedged his bets, writing: 'Most followers of the sport would expect India to do an encore [after the 1983 Prudential World Cup victory] and steal the thunder! But coming as it does a good 18 months after India pulled the rug from under the West Indies, we cannot consider ourselves hot favourites.'

Vengsarkar did not even mention India's spin bowlers, instead focusing on the medium pacers. The same was the case with the experienced R. Mohan in *Sportstar* preview special,[19] where he virtually wrote off India's chances: 'Objectively speaking, India has less chance of stunning the cricket world in Melbourne than it had in the World Cup. The simple reasoning is, we have come down so much it appears we do not even have the capacity to dream again.'

Only S. Venkataraghavan, who had captained India in the 1975 and 1979 Prudential World Cups, in his article in the same issue[20] focused on Siva: 'Indian selectors will have to be complimented for their decision in including young Siva for the Australian tour. Being a wrist spinner he could do better in Australia with the wickets having more bounce and pace. Pakistan has used Abdul Qadir successfully in one-dayers.'

It's now part of Indian cricket folklore that Siva was the leading bowler in the WCC, and with Shastri in tandem, spin was the winner for India. The leggie bowled 48 of his 50-over quota in the five matches, while Shastri was the only bowler of all the seven teams to complete his full quota of 50. Siva topped the tournament with 10 wickets, while Shastri bagged eight.

---

[19] R. Mohan, 'The Beginning of a New Dream', *Sportstar*, 16 February 1985
[20] S. Venkataraghavan, 'The Right Approach for Instant Cricket', *Sportstar*, 16 February 1985

Shastri also scored three 50s and had 182 runs at 45.50. His opening partner Srikkanth also scored three 50s with a highest of 93 not out and 238 runs at 59.50.

But after the final, where Pakistan were beaten by eight wickets, it was Shastri who was named Champion of Champions, the term used in this event for the Man of the Tournament, and drove away with the grand prize of the golden Audi 100 luxury car, valued at over $A40,000. According to the Channel Nine guide to the tournament, it had recently been voted World Car of the Year: 'It is the most valuable individual cricket award ever offered...fitted with climate-controlled air conditioning, power steering, power windows, AM/FM stereo cassette, 5-cylinder fuel injected engine and plush interior.'

Quite a package for any Indian, whose idea of a luxury car back then was the boxy Maruti Suzuki 800!

However, it was not a popular choice. If the fans had a vote, they would have gone with Srikkanth, who blazed a trail with his aggressive strokes, scoring his runs at the strike rate of 79.60 and was Man of the Match in the final for his 67 from 77 balls, strike rate 87.01, which was phenomenal at the time, when any total over 200 was considered challenging. Shastri's 63 not out came from 148 balls at the sedate SR of 42.57.

Shastri's role was well defined—to hold one end up while Srikkanth took on the attacking role, as he had always done. Shastri was perhaps unfairly criticized for playing it safe, as his tournament SR of 49.32 showed. But his percentage game, combined with his bowling, was enough for the panel of five commentators from the Channel Nine team to make their pick.

Shastri won the Man of the Match award against Australia and in the semifinal versus New Zealand, while Srikkanth was also Man of the Match against England, apart from the final. India's opening tie against Pakistan was won by six wickets, with Azharuddin winning the Man of the Match with 93 not out. The choice of Shastri against Australia was most surprising. He scored 51 and took one wicket, while Srikkanth remained unbeaten on 93 from just 115 deliveries, the joint top score in the tournament. Srikkanth being passed over for the award in this match also rankled with the fans, for whom the irrepressible 'Cheekah'—top scorer in the 1983 Prudential World Cup final with 38—was always a crowd favourite. Even Gavaskar picked Srikkanth as the best batsman of the tournament.

Shastri, always frank to the point of being blunt, made no bones that he had one eye on the big prize right from the start. He was surely not the only one. In fact, on the eve of the final, there were three in the running for the glittering German-made Audi—Shastri, Srikkanth and Pakistan's Mudassar Nazar, who, like Shastri, had done well with both bat and ball.

Today, Shastri is perhaps the most-trolled Indian cricketer on social media, with Sanjay Manjrekar not far behind. But long before social media was invented, Shastri earned the tag of a 'selfish' cricketer, and the angry crowd chants of 'Shastri hai hai', which were first heard in the third Test against England at Calcutta just three months earlier (he crawled to 111 in 455 minutes), now became a staple wherever he played.

Asked if the label of 'Champion of Champions' given to Shastri was justified, Imran Khan said in an interview to *Sportsworld* (1–7 May 1985):

Well, we are talking about a certain moment in time. I don't think it would be fair to call him 'Champion of Champions', though on the other hand, let me say that the way he used the conditions as a bowler and played the anchor role as a batsman, he deserved the award completely. He has got the temperament to be the future captain of India.

Shastri, Siva, Roger Binny, Kapil and Madan Lal bowled so brilliantly that in every match, save for the final where Pakistan lost nine wickets, the Indians bowled out the opposition.

Apart from the bowling, a major factor in India's victory, as acknowledged by the skipper, was the presence of Sadanand Viswanath behind the stumps. His lightning reflexes and constant encouragement to the bowlers helped lift the spirits of the Indians. Most Indian wicketkeepers preferred to go about their task unobtrusively, Farokh Engineer being an exception. But to have an Indian 'keeper chattering away behind the stumps was a revelation, and was calculated to rile the batsmen too.

One batsman who was irritated in the final was Pakistan captain Javed Miandad—ironical since he was notorious for his chatter while fielding. At the drinks break, he complained to Gavaskar, telling him, '*Insaan khel rahe hain, jaanwar nahin.*' (Human beings are playing, not animals.) As narrated in Gavaskar's book *One-Day Wonders*, given Miandad's reputation, Gavaskar could scarcely believe his ears and 'laughed in his face.'

Rattled, Miandad fell to the Sadanand/Siva combine. In Gavaskar's words:

> Siva worked his magic, flighting the ball, inviting Javed to step out and pitching it perfectly so it spun away and beat Javed's bat. In a flash, Vish had the bails off, running towards the square leg umpire to confirm the dismissal, then running towards the bowler and still finding time in between to mouth two words that told Javed what to do.

Some chutzpah this, for a youngster in his maiden international tournament, against a grizzled veteran. The footage of the dismissal, 35 years later, is still one of the most-watched among Indian cricket fans. Years later, in New Delhi during a Test match, Siva, now a TV commentator, told me that this is the only tape in his collection.

In an interview to *Sportsworld* (27 March–2 April 1985) Siva had this to say about the master delivery:

> Well, Miandad was coming down the track quite often. I knew I could not beat him in flight because he has good footwork. I knew I had to beat him by turn. So for that I gave a particularly hard tweak and as he came down the wicket he was beaten by the break. The ball floated past him and Viswanath did the rest.

Viswanath had also excelled in the group match versus England at Sydney, which India won by 86 runs. He had five dismissals (three catches and two stumpings) and it would have been fitting if he had been awarded the Man of the Match.

I once asked left arm spinner Maninder Singh who, in his opinion, was the best Indian wicketkeeper during his career. He thought for a moment and said, 'Sadanand Viswanath.' They toured Sri Lanka together in 1985, in what would be the only three Tests in Sadanand's career, the last of his 22 ODIs coming in 1988.

Sadly, Siva, Maninder and Sadanand, once touted as the future of Indian cricket, ended up being part of its lost generation instead. They all had their battles with personal demons and, as a result, played a grand total of just 47 Tests and 97 ODIs, despite being supremely talented. Thankfully, today they are involved in the game they love so much in one capacity or the other, though their playing careers were sadly truncated.

The doyen of cricket writers, John Woodcock expressed his delight in the introduction to the *World Championship of Cricket Limited Edition* released by the Victorian Cricket

Association, the hosts of the event: 'Shastri was revealed as an outstanding all-rounder, and the batsman everyone wanted to see was Azharuddin; Siva, in partnership with Shastri, struck a splendid blow for the spin bowling fraternity.'

Writing in *Sportstar* victory special (30 March 1985), Bob Simpson, no mean leg spinner himself, wrote:

> For a player of such tender years, Siva has oodles of talent and a wonderful temperament. I never go overboard at the first sight of any player but the tiny leg spinner earned my admiration with his incredible spirit under pressure. He has a lovely high action, clever variation and the ability to bowl both line and length even when under assault.

And while Kohli believes, as is the popular perception, that aggression and fighting spirit entered Indian cricket's lexicon only from 2000 under Ganguly's leadership, here's what Simpson wrote: 'I particularly liked the aggression showed by India on the field. So often I have felt that the Indians have almost been apologizing and sometimes been bullied into mistakes. Not this group, and they took the fight to the opposition with boldness, flair, great skill and confidence.'

Siva himself was all praise for his skipper, allowing him to set his own field, despite the huge disparity in experience between bowler and captain; this, he said, boosted his confidence.

Manager E.A.S. Prasanna also had a major role to play in the triumph. The master off spinner even bowled in the nets. Gavaskar joked that he was tempted to include him in the team, save for his fielding! Prasanna laid to rest the myth of spinners not being effective in limited-over cricket in an interview to Mohan in the *Sportstar* victory special:

The presence of two spinners gave the right kind of balance to our attack. No other country had this and we were fortunate to be able to command such a weapon in limited overs cricket. I am sure this sounds strange, but spinners can contribute substantially even in the so-called instant cricket.

The Indian victory and the master move by the selectors— Bishan Singh Bedi among them—to go in for two specialist spinners and their leading role in the tournament, changed the face of one-day cricket forever. The floodgates were now open and the likes of Anil Kumble, Shane Warne, Muttiah Muralitharan, Harbhajan Singh and so many others should be indebted to the Indian selectors and captain for busting the myth once and for all. Their presence has relieved the tedium of pace and more pace, and brought in a new and fascinating facet to this form of the game, which was just 14 years old at the time of the WCC. Now, in 2021, it will celebrate its 50th birthday.

On his return to Bombay, Gavaskar had an answer for those who maintained that the victory in the Prudential World Cup had been a fluke. 'This is the age of sequel movies. We had *Rocky One,* we had *Rocky Two* and then we had *Jaws One, Jaws Two.* Now there is one more addition to the genre. Fluke One, Fluke Two.'

Iconic Moment

The sight of the Indian team piling into and onto Shastri's newly won Audi, as he drove round the massive MCG, is one of Indian cricket's iconic moments. To be chosen as the best from among 98 cricketers from around the world, was a great honour.

Indian sportspersons have quite a story with their luxury cars. Before the Audi, there was the Volvo, won by one of India's tennis greats, Vijay Amritraj. He beat Jimmy Connors 7-5, 2-6, 7-5 in the final of the Volvo International tournament in Bretton Woods, New Hampshire, USA for his first major international title. At the time, the car was valued at $7,000, which was approximately ₹56,000—a princely sum. He also won $5,000 in prize money. The 360 per cent import duty was eventually waived by the government.

In 2002, Sachin Tendulkar was gifted a Ferrari-360 Modena by Fiat, whose cars he was endorsing (they are part of the same firm), for equaling Don Bradman's 29 Test centuries the year earlier in West Indies. They arranged for F1 legend Michael Schumacher to hand over the keys to Tendulkar at Silverstone during the tour of England. The government waived the import duty of ₹1.13 crores (as they had done with the Volvo and Audi too) on the car, worth approximately ₹75 lakh. This unleashed a storm of protests and public interest litigations, and Fiat eventually paid the duty.

Watching the WCC final at his home in Madras on that Sunday evening, my sports editor at *The Indian Express*, Rajan Bala (who passed away in 2009) was getting increasingly frustrated. The newspaper had decided not to send a correspondent to Australia, while R. Mohan of *The Hindu*, who had also reported the Prudential World Cup two years earlier, was one of the few Indian reporters Down Under.

A prolific writer with a fine turn of phrase and sound technical knowledge, Bala could not sit still. He decided that he had to write a report of the final for the Southern editions of the daily. But how? He could not use his own name, so he came up with what he claimed was a variation of his full name, Natarajan Balasubramaniam.

Imagine the surprise of the readers when they opened their newspapers the next morning, to see a name no one in the cricket or journalistic world had heard of before (or since): A.A.J. Tanner. So, finally after 35 years, it can be revealed—the mysterious A.A.J. Tanner was actually Rajan Bala!

Crowning Glory

Barely did the players have time to return home, be with their families and celebrate their victory in what has become known as the mini World Cup, when it was back to Sharjah, where a year earlier they had lifted the Asia Cup.

And just 12 days after the 10 March WCC final, India and Pakistan were up against each other again in the Rothmans four-nation tournament.

It was India's 75th ODI and the 321st overall. Now, with 4,223 ODIs having been played till the end of 2019, it still remains a world record for lowest total successfully defended in a full match, 125 runs. Imran turned in one of the all-time great spells of hostile fast swing bowling, 6 for 14 in eight overs, and the Pakistan players and supporters among the full house were super confident that it would be a cakewalk for them.

In the Indian dressing room, skipper Kapil exhorted his players to fight for every run, telling them that they should prove they are worthy world champions.

With Kapil (3-17) leading the way, the bowlers saw to it that Pakistan crumbled to 87 all out in 32.5 overs, with five batsmen failing to score, including skipper Miandad and Imran. Shastri and Siva were in the thick of things again with two wickets each, and the miracle at Lord's was now repeated at Sharjah. Gavaskar at slip was at his best, pouching four catches.

For Imran, the Man of the Match award meant little, and

he admitted that it was one of the hardest defeats in his career to stomach.

With England falling by the wayside, it was India versus Australia in the final. Like most matches at Sharjah, it was low scoring, Australia's 139 all out being overhauled by India for the loss of seven wickets.

From June 1983 to March 1985, India had won four titles on the trot on foreign soil. From London to Melbourne to Sharjah, the Indians were unbeatable in tournaments, even as they succumbed in bilateral series at home.

Kapil himself was convinced that India were now the number one ODI side in the world, even above West Indies. This was echoed by Tiger Pataudi. But what was behind the reversal of the trend of winning at home and losing abroad?

Gavaskar, Kapil, Shastri and Prasanna were all on the same page on this one. Playing at home before the demanding fans and the media put added strain on the players. Abroad, the pressures and scrutiny were less invasive, allowing the players to play free of tension. Further, the outfields, particularly in England and Australia, were lush and green and made diving much less hazardous than in India, where the grounds tend to be hard and abrasive. The Indian fielding was top class right through this golden period, and Kapil, speaking after the four-nation win, was convinced that this was the deciding factor. (*Sportsworld*, 10–16 April 1985)

> Fielding was the most constant and crucial factor in India's climb from the bottom of the cricketing world four years ago to the very top today. I would like to hear anyone place the West Indies ahead of us now. Do we have to do anything more to prove that we are number one?

Gavaskar also pointed to the pitches in England, which aid

swing, and in Australia, the extra bounce was helpful to the Indian bowling attack. At home, the tracks were batting friendly, blunting India's bowling. The huge boundaries in Australia back then, stretching from 90 to 100 yards (no longer the case) meant that it was extremely difficult for the batsmen to hit Siva to the boundary, even when he bowled quite a few full tosses.

From the first match at the Asia Cup in 1984 till the final one in 2000, India and Pakistan played 24 ODIs in the UAE capital. India won the first two in 1984 and 1985, but the tables turned after that and Pakistan dominated, winning 18 times out of the 24.

From 1974 till the final of the Rothmans Cup in March 1985, India had played 76 ODIs, winning 30, losing 43 with three no-results. But the lopsidedness came in the home and away record—Played: 23; Won: 8; Lost: 13; No Result: 2 at home. Abroad, it was considerably better: P: 53: W: 22: L: 33: NR: 1.

All this is quite a different scenario from what has been prevailing in Indian cricket over the past decade, and indeed for most of its history. But one thing is sure—neither did Indian cricket begin in 1971, nor in 2000.

11

AND FINALLY...

My career has been glorious for myself and hopefully for the spectators too.

—Salim Durani

Some Indian cricketers inspire admiration, Sunil Gavaskar being a prime example; some like Kapil Dev inspire awe; one—Sachin Tendulkar—even worship. But I can think of just two in Indian cricket's storied history that inspired adoration, even love.

Salim Aziz Durani and G.R. Viswanath fit comfortably into this category. And while a number of cricketers of royal stock have represented India in Test cricket (Chapter 5), including two Nawabs who captained, for those of a particular generation there can only be one 'Prince' Salim.

Tall, gaunt, green-eyed and with dashing matinee idol looks—appropriate in Durani's case since he acted in a film (*Charitra*, meaning character, co-starring Parveen Babi)—he lit up the 1960s with his silken batting, brilliant left-arm spin and dashing presence. He had an insouciant air as well, that perhaps gave the impression of being casual in his approach.

Genius is an overworked term in sport. But if you ask his contemporaries to sum him up in one word, it is 'genius' that you will hear almost unanimously.

The Bengal and East Zone captain of the 1970s, Raju Mukherji has written glowingly of Durani in his book *Cricket in India: Origin and Heroes*, in a chapter dripping with admiration and affection. Teammate or rival, fan or journalist, Durani inspired such feelings in almost one and all.

One of the few exceptions was one of his captains, 'Tiger' Pataudi, who always felt that Durani did not do full justice to his enormous talents. In an interview to Sambit Bal in *Wisden Asia Cricket*,[21] March 2002), Pataudi when asked how he would deal with 'difficult cricketers', replied, more in regret than in anger:

> Every team has a couple of difficult characters—in my time there were a few. Salim Durani was one. I felt I couldn't handle him properly...I felt I couldn't get the best out of him. He was an extremely talented cricketer—who lacked a certain amount of cricketing discipline. We tried to organize it—me and a few other senior cricketers. But we didn't succeed. He did well, but a man of his talent could have been made to perform better.

Durani, in reaction, rated Pataudi as the best of his captains and added that he (Durani) was solely responsible for all his performances, good or otherwise. The dashing Nawab and the

---

[21]Sambit Bal, 'A Bad Captain Can Make a Great Team Look Ordinary', *Wisden Asia Cricket*, March 2002

handsome Pathan were perhaps never on the same wavelength.

So versatile was Durani that he started his career as a wicketkeeper, then became a spinner, then a batsman and finally an all-rounder! He had earlier represented Gujarat and Saurashtra, but it was for Rajasthan and Central Zone that he chalked up his feats in domestic cricket which are the stuff of legend.

Rare Talent

Constantly in and out of the team, often in mid-series, the fact that Durani played a mere 29 Tests from his debut in 1959–60 to his final Test in 1972–73 means that Indian cricket was denied the services of a rare talent. Sadly, even after brilliant performances, he would quickly find himself on the sidelines. But his bowling record of 75 wickets is stellar. His most iconic feat remains bowling the great Garry Sobers first ball and then claiming the precious wicket of Clive Lloyd too in the second innings of the second Test at Port of Spain, Trinidad in 1971— two magical deliveries that virtually sealed India's first victory over West Indies. He had other match-winning feats with the ball too.

Ajit Wadekar, his last Test captain, in his book *My Cricketing Years*, variously described Durani as gifted, temperamental and moody. It was this seemingly casual attitude that may have made him difficult to handle, both for his captains and the selectors.

But is that casual tag another myth? Sunil Gavaskar—who till this day calls Durani 'Daddy', such is his respect and affection for this father figure—wrote in *Sunny Days*:

Salim has been a much misunderstood man. He has been

called moody and this stigma has stuck to him. But this is not a correct estimate of the man. He treats a Test match as he would treat a club game. He is a crowd-puller, first and last. He is often accused of not taking Test cricket seriously. This is equally untrue. I recall during the 1971 West Indies tour when Salim was failing with the bat after a dazzling beginning how upset he was about his form... People call him a wayward genius. I don't know about his being wayward, but he is certainly a genius. A genius whom the authorities have never bothered to understand.

So, how did Durani feel about this sensitive issue? In an interview with Ayaz Memon,[22] when asked why his record did not reflect his talent, he was candid: 'Yes, I should have made more runs [1,202 runs at 25.04 with one century and seven fifties] but I lacked patience and frequently threw my wicket away when I had the bowlers at my mercy.'

There are so many mysteries and myths surrounding Durani that he must surely be a biographer's dream. In fact, that is another recurring myth—the biography/autobiography that is due any day! So often have I heard this story over the years and yet, now, in his late 80s and with failing physical health and memory, it may be too late.

As far back as 1973, he was claiming in an interview[23] that the book was in the works and he even had a title for it—*Ask for the Six*. It never happened of course. And even Gavaskar in his book published in 1976 sounded skeptical: 'I don't know if he will ever write it, but I do hope he does.'

The title reflects another of the stories circulating around Durani, aka Mr Sixer—that he could hit sixes on demand into

---

[22]Ayaz Memon, 'Mr. Sixer', *Cricketer Asia*, July 1983
[23]*Sportsweek*, 22 July 1973

the exact place in the stands where cries of 'We want sixer!' would ring out around grounds in India. Far-fetched perhaps, but 15 sixes in 50 innings was an impressive strike rate, at a time when Indian batsmen were not famed for their big hitting. Even in his final series against England at home in 1972–73, when close to 40, Durani in just three Tests hit more sixes (seven) than the rest of the team put together (four).

Kabuliwallah?

The most recurring myth though surrounds his place of birth. Like many Indians, Durani too is not sure of his exact date of birth, but he has stuck to 11 December 1934 as his 'official' date. But where was he born?

For years, a staple of cricket quizzes has been to name the Indian Test cricketers born outside India—Lall Singh (Kuala Lumpur, Malaysia); Ashok Gandotra (Rio de Janeiro, Brazil); Rabindra Ramanarayan 'Robin' Singh (Princes Town, Trinidad); and Salim Durani (Kabul, Afghanistan).

However, Durani himself has sought, over the years, to dispel this myth. He has said in interviews that his father Abdul Aziz Durani was born in Kabul in 1905, where he was in the dry fruits business, whereas his paternal grandparents were originally from Karachi. Other reports claim that Aziz was born in Jhelum, near Rawalpindi. The exact year is also not clear, either 1905 or 1910.

His father played one unofficial Test for India as a wicketkeeper/batsman versus Jack Ryder's Australian side at Calcutta in 1935–36. He was also a member of the Nawanagar team (now merged with Saurashtra) that won the Ranji Trophy in 1936–37, opening the batting with Vinoo Mankad.

However, at the time of Partition in 1947, 'Master Aziz'

as he came to be known, left his family behind in Gujarat and moved to the new nation of Pakistan, where he became a famed coach of the famous Mohammad brothers (Wazir, Raees, Hanif, Mushtaq and Sadiq), Javed Miandad and many others. Sadly, he died in 1979, destitute and forgotten. Why he left his family behind is more a mystery than a myth and left a deep emotional scar both on the father and his children. Reportedly, Salim met his father only once after the separation and that was in India in 1960.

Salim has stated that he was born 'under the open skies' ('which is why I have always played my cricket with freedom,' he has joked) when his mother went into labour and gave birth while they were travelling in a camel caravan from Karachi to Kabul, in the region of the Khyber Pass—but not in Kabul. When he was three years old, the family moved to Gujarat.

Salim's birth reminds me of the feisty character Beatrice in William Shakespeare's play *Much Ado About Nothing*: 'There was a star danced, and under that was I born.'

It should be recalled here that the Khyber Pass, which is in the Northwest of Pakistan, was then part of undivided India. Those Indian cricketers, born before 1947 in areas that became part of Pakistan after Partition, are not considered to be foreign-born.

Durani spoke about the details surrounding his birth to veteran sports journalist Rameshwar Singh in Jaipur in May 2004 for an interview in the Hindi daily *Rajasthan Patrika*. 'Salim bhai, however, quite enjoys the tag of being the first Kabul-born Test cricketer, so has not really bothered to clarify this further,' Singh told me. Indeed, this myth has passed into cricket folklore and even into the record books.

In an interview in *Sportstar* (9 January 2021) shortly after his 86th birthday, he told G. Viswanath:

I was not born in Kabul. In fact I have never visited. My parents and *bade abba* (grandfather) belong to Kabul...The entire Durani family moved to Karachi in the second half of the 1930s...I don't remember much about Karachi. I was born in 1934 and must have come to Jamnagar much before the partition of undivided India. My father, mother and all other family members moved to Jamnagar.

In June 2018, when Afghanistan played their maiden Test at Bengaluru, the BCCI invited Durani as their special guest. No one questioned where he had actually been born, since his roots lie in Kabul and that is where he spent the first three years of his life, though he has never been back. It was an emotional occasion, as the Afghan cricketers and administrators rushed to greet him and the occasion gave the ageing veteran perhaps his last time in the sun.

Durani has suffered vicissitudes both in his playing and family life. But he has no regrets, holds no rancor or grudges against anyone. He closed the interview with Memon in *Cricketer Asia* with this sentiment: 'My career has been glorious for myself and hopefully for the spectators too. My opportunities were limited. I spent five years in the wilderness and then later two years again. These were the best years of my life. But then there are no regrets that I have.'

What better way to end than to quote from the chapter on Durani from Raju Mukherji's book?

Salim Aziz Durani will always remain an idol for me and a hero to people who value class, confidence, courage and character. He was an artist as well as a sculpture, a genius as well as a monument, loved and respected at the same time.

Buggy and that Kiss

The Hyderabad Ranji Trophy team of the 1960s and 70s was one of the most charismatic in the history of Indian domestic cricket. This is no hyperbole. It had in its ranks, after all, the stylish M.L. Jaisimha as captain, the dashing Nawab Mansur Ali Khan Pataudi (after he shifted from the cesspool of Delhi cricket)—India's skipper but only too happy to play under his great buddy Jai's captaincy both for Hyderabad and South Zone—and the debonair Abbas Ali Baig. They never won the big prize, but as one of their stalwarts once said, they certainly had the most fun.

For Indian cricket fans of my generation, this was a golden age and not necessarily for results on the field of play. These three, along with Salim Durani, Farokh Engineer, Budhi Kunderan and others, brought style and panache to Indian cricket, which till then was not famed for flamboyance. As the saying goes, women wanted to be with them, men (and boys) wanted to be like them.

Of the 'Three Musketeers' of Hyderabad cricket, Baig (aka Buggy) had the shortest international career—just 10 Test matches from 1959 to 1967. But, he had the most spectacular start and is the last of the three still with us.

Born just 16 days apart in 1939, both Jaisimha (the older) and Baig made their Test debuts on the wretched 1959 tour of England, the first time India had suffered a whitewash (5-0), Jaisimha in the second Test at Lord's and Baig in the fourth at Old Trafford, Manchester.

Baig was called up by the team management as a replacement for the injured Vijay Manjrekar, while he was a 20-year-old freshman at Oxford University (the Board indulged in cradle snatching, he once told me with a smile) and marked his debut with a delightful century—about the only bright spot for India in the dire series. That made him the fourth Indian to achieve the feat, the first outside India and, for nearly 60 years, the youngest too.

In the 1959–60 season that followed, he played three Tests against the visiting Australians and it was at the Brabourne Stadium, Bombay in the third Test that began on New Year's Day 1960, where an incident occurred that placed a spotlight on Baig that even 60 years later sees his name pop up on social media.

Baig scored 50 in the first innings, with Australia gaining a lead of 98 runs. On the final day (6 January), India was struggling at 112 for 4, just 14 runs ahead, before Baig and Ramnath Kenny added 109 runs to take them to safety, with Baig scoring his second fifty of the match.

Sensation and Scandal

The pair were heading to the pavilion at tea when a young lady jumped the fencing, ran up and standing on tiptoes, gave the surprised batsman a peck on the cheek. It was a sensational incident in front of a packed house, including the young Abbas' parents, and would become enshrined in popular culture thanks to Salman Rusdhie's novel *The Moor's Last Sigh* and an 80s TV ad for *Cadbury's* chocolates. Back then, it caused something of both a scandal and a sensation, though it was just an innocent peck.

'We were surrounded by a crowd of fans and photographers as we walked off. Suddenly, this young lady rushed up to me. It all happened in a flash,' Baig told me in an interview that appeared in *Hindustan Times* on 6 January 2020, the 60th anniversary.

The myth and mystery surrounds the identity of the young lady in question. Numerous efforts over the years have failed to crack the case. What I can confirm though is that she was a 20-year-old college student from the Parsi community. This was conveyed to me by Nari Contractor via his son Hoshedar. Contractor excelled in the Test with 108 and 43, and is himself Parsi. The story goes that she did it based on a bet with her college friends. There are four Indian survivors from that match, apart from Contractor and Baig himself— Chandu Borde and Durani being the other two. If she were to be alive today, she would be around the same age as the object of her affection.

The famous photo, widely circulated and commented upon on social media, shows the lady in question in a black skirt, barefoot, her face obscured and a smile on Baig's face even as his head is lowered.

All the more surprising then that the former UN diplomat, Congress MP and author Shashi Tharoor should identify her as a 'sari-clad' Hindu in the 2009 book *Shadows Across the Playing Field: 60 Years of India-Pakistan Cricket*, jointly written with the Pakistan diplomat and cricket administrator Shaharyar Khan.

Tharoor emphasized that Baig was a Muslim and his admirer Hindu. He repeated the myth of the 'sari-clad lovely' in an article in *Sportstar* dated 15 March 2018, despite the evidence in the famous photo.

Another myth, much more damaging and in fact a canard, followed Baig's failure in the home series against Pakistan in 1960-61, where he scored just 34 runs from four innings in the first three Tests, after which he was dropped for the next two.

Baig revealed to author James Astill that he had received hate mail, accusing him of deliberately underperforming. 'I was flabbergasted,' Baig recalled. 'I mean, it hadn't even occurred to one that anyone could connect my poor form to my being a Muslim.'[24]

Baig was recalled for two Tests in the 1966–67 home series versus West Indies and also toured England in 1971 without playing in the Test series. His 10 Tests with 428 runs at 23.77 is not a true reflection of the class of this elegant stroke-player.

Across the border, the attitude to Indian Muslims playing, captaining and excelling in cricket, or for that matter in any sport, is not taken well. The best (or worst) illustration of this is the tasteless comment by Omar Noman (a former UN diplomat, no less) in his history of Pakistan cricket.[25]

Noman condemns Ghulam Ahmed for helping to draw the fifth Test match against Pakistan at Calcutta in December 1952, in partnership with debutant centurion Deepak Shodhan, simply because of Ahmed's faith.

Ahmed, a Hyderabadi like Baig, was a future captain of India, a skillful off spinner, a thorough gentleman and one of Indian cricket's great administrators, being the chairman of selectors who picked the winning team for the 1983 Prudential World Cup. As Tharoor put it in his book, it is this narrow-minded attitude that 'betrays the vast gulf in the mindset of the two nations'.

This same narrow-mindedness was displayed by Pakistan's captain Shoaib Malik (who would later marry Indian tennis ace Sania Mirza), after India had won the inaugural ICC World T20 championship in Johannesburg in September 2007. In his post-final speech, Malik apologized to Muslims 'all over the world'

---

[24]James Astill, *The Great Tamasha: Cricket, Corruption and the Turbulent Rise of Modern India*, Bloomsbury Publishing Plc, 1st edition, 2013 (extract used with kind permission of publisher)
[25]Omar Noman, *Pride and Passion: An Exhilarating Half Century of Cricket in Pakistan*, Oxford University Press, 1998

for the defeat, even as Man of the Match Irfan Pathan—who ironically counted Malik among his three wickets—was fuming just a few feet away. Irfan's elder half-brother Yusuf made his international debut in this landmark match.

A famed cricket historian told me some years back that when India toured Pakistan in 1978 after a gap of 20 years, the Pakistani commentators never used the first name of Indian wicketkeeper Syed Kirmani, as his surname could be mistaken for either a Sindhi or even Parsi name.

In fact, when it comes to minorities in Test cricket, India has a record it can be proud of, far superior to that of Pakistan. A total of 34 Muslims have played for India out of 296 Test cricketers, till the end of 2019. Of these, four have led the country—Iftikhar Ali Khan (the Nawab of Pataudi Sr.), Ghulam Ahmed, Mansur Ali Khan (the Nawab of Pataudi Jr.) and Mohammad Azharuddin, who in addition also captained India in the 1996 and 1999 World Cups. Syed Kirmani too captained in one ODI.

In addition to that, two Christians (Vijay Samuel Hazare and Borde), two Parsis (Polly Umrigar and Contractor) and a Sikh (Bishan Singh Bedi) have captained India in Test cricket.

On 22 November 2006, during the second ODI between India and South Africa at Durban, I received a call from a Mumbai Urdu daily, asking if this was the first time four Muslims were in an Indian cricket team. Apart from Mohammad Kaif, Munaf Patel, Zaheer Khan and Wasim Jaffer, a fifth, Irfan Pathan, was also part of the touring party but not in the playing XI.

I advised the caller to have a look at the scorecard for the very first Test match played by India at Lord's in 1932. Captained by C.K. Nayudu, the playing XI consisted of four Muslims, two Parsis and a Sikh. In the 1936 Oval Test, there were six and in the second unofficial Test at Calcutta, versus

Jack Ryder's Australians in 1935–36, there were as many as seven in the playing XI. The numbers dropped understandably post-Partition in 1947, with the creation of Pakistan.

The newspaper's headline the day after the Durban ODI said it all: *'Hindustan one-day team mein pehlee baar chaar Musalmaan ek saath.'* ('For the first time four Muslims in India's ODI team.')

Blowing His Own Trumpet!

Farokh Engineer—in the 60s and 70s, the name spelt magic for cricket lovers in India and around the world. Flamboyant with the bat and agile with the big gloves, he had a huge fan following who adored his style and panache.

Engineer is not the first and certainly not the last among many famous sportspersons to embellish his own deeds with colourful stories which have entered cricket folklore and are accepted by many as gospel truth. Some of those tales are apocryphal, some perhaps figments of an active imagination and many merely made-up—the master of myths!

When county cricket opened up for professionals from around the world in 1968, Engineer joined the likes of Garry Sobers as among the first to join the circuit and add a dash of colour and excitement to the staid scene. In Lancashire, the county he represented with distinction till 1976, he is loved as one of their own.

Now in his eighties, he continues to make regular visits to his birthplace of Mumbai, to which he retains a strong emotional attachment and where he has a legion of fans and friends.

Engineer made his Test debut against England at Kanpur in 1962, just three years after his maiden first-class match. For some years, it would be a game of musical chairs with his great friend and rival Budhi Kunderan—with K.S. Indrajitsinhji playing a cameo role in between—for a place in the Indian team, before Engineer cemented his place in early 1967.

Test Debut

Engineer, unusually for an Indian cricketer, has two authorized autobiographies of his life and career, both written by English writers. This is largely because he made such a name for himself in county cricket. The first, published in 2004, titled *Farokh Engineer: From the Far Pavilion*, and written by John Cantrell, is full of Eastern exotica and stereotypes. The second, *Farokh: The Cricketing Cavalier* by Colin Evans, was published in 2016 and lays more emphasis on his exploits for Lancashire.

And it is at Kanpur on debut where Engineer's fanciful tales begin—in fact from the very first deliveries he faced in his Test career!

In 2018 at Trent Bridge, when wicketkeeper Rishabh Pant became the first Indian to get off the mark on Test debut with a six from the second ball he faced from leg-spinner Adil Rashid, Engineer told *Hindustan Times* (27 August 2018): 'I'm very impressed, he has tremendous reflexes. I love to see youngsters make a mark. He didn't show any nerves and hit the second ball for a six. My first three balls I faced in Test cricket, I hit them for fours, but that was out of sheer nervousness.'

Except, that is not what happened. And the bowler he faced first up was not Tony Lock as he claims in both the books, but pace bowler Barry Knight, who had taken the wicket of A.G. Kripal Singh with the fifth ball of the over. Engineer got a single from that final delivery and then, in the next over from pace bowler David Brown, he got a single and then failed to score off the third ball he faced.

So, no boundaries at the start of his Test career. How do we know? Thanks to the diligence of Melbourne-based Australian statistician Charles Davis and his superb website sportstats. com.au. Davis has obtained the ball-by-ball details for the vast majority of all Test matches since the first at Melbourne in 1877, though there are some vital ones missing. The scorebooks for the 1961–62 home series against England, won 2-0 by India, and many others are with the MCC library at Lord's, though details for the first Test at Bombay are not available.

Engineer played in the first three Tests of the 1962 tour of West Indies, which immediately followed his debut. India were whitewashed 5-0 and this forced the BCCI's hands. For the 1962–63 domestic season, they imported four fast bowlers from the Caribbean in a bid to test our players against genuine pace which was woefully lacking in Indian cricket at the time. The quartet was assigned to four different state sides and zones for the Ranji and Duleep Trophy, namely Roy Gilchrist (Hyderabad/South Zone), Lester King (Bengal/East), Charlie Stayers (Bombay/West) and Chester Watson (Delhi/North). It was the choice of Gilchrist that raised eyebrows, since he had played his last Test in India in December 1959 and had gained a highly controversial reputation due to his wild temper and also been called for chucking.

In the books, Engineer claims that he affected a smart leg side stumping from one of the fastest bowlers of his time, which he states enraged 'Gilly'. In Engineer's narration, it happened in the final of the Moin-ud-Dowlah tournament in Hyderabad in October 1962, for M.A. Chidambaram's XI against Associated Cement Company XI.

But, it never happened! Engineer took just one catch in the match, in the first innings off the bowling of King. Another myth busted!

World Record—Not!

When Garry Sobers brought his mighty West Indies team for a short tour in 1966–67, another whitewash was predicted. India fought hard before losing the first Test at Bombay, were well beaten in the second at Calcutta and had much the better of the drawn third at Madras. Kunderan kept wickets in the first two Tests and, despite a good run of batting form, was dropped at Madras.

In 1986, shortly after Viv Richards recorded the fastest Test century in history in terms of balls received (56) against England, I received a letter from my cricket guru in England, famed cricket historian and author David Frith.

Frith said that he had been approached by Engineer with a request to try to trace the scorebook for the Madras Test, as he was sure that his century in the first innings (109) had been scored from just 47 balls. I was living in Madras at that time and working with *The Indian Express*, but when I approached the Tamil Nadu Cricket Association (the staging association), I drew a blank. There was no trace of the scorebook. It was the first time that I had heard of this story and I was intrigued, so I asked around in the cricket circles in Madras but got no answers.

Without access to the scorebook and long before the advent of the Internet and online cricket databases, I had to tell Frith that no evidence existed.

Richards' record was first equaled by Misbah-ul-Haq and finally beaten by Brendon McCullum (54) against Australia in 2016.

As already noted in this chapter, there are a number of Test matches for which details of balls faced do not exist, and this is one of them. So, what is the story of this remarkable innings and what are the myths that have lingered over it for more than half a century?

India batted first and Engineer opened with Dilip Sardesai. What is not in dispute is that by lunch on the opening day, Engineer had reached 94 and the partnership was 125 runs from 28 overs.

That meant Engineer fell just six short of becoming only the fourth batsman after Victor Trumper, Charlie Macartney and Don Bradman (all Australians), to reach a century before lunch on the first day of a Test match. Three others have followed since, including India's Shikhar Dhawan.

In a column appearing under his name in an *Outlook* magazine special issue in 2007, marking 75 years of Indian Test cricket, Engineer wrote: '...the century I got off 47 balls against the West Indies at Chennai is merely a reflection of how seriously I took my batting.' In the same column, he claims that his Test average was higher than Pataudi's and Wadekar's (Engineer: 31.08; Wadekar: 31.07; Pataudi: 34.91).

Sadly, the scorebook for the entire series is not available. Hence, one cannot be sure of the number of balls Engineer faced to reach his 100. Here is what Charles Davis wrote in his blog on 5 January 2017:

I don't have any scorebook for this Test. However, 46 balls (I have also read 48 balls) is effectively impossible. For one thing, in reality Engineer took 23 minutes and (probably) eight overs after lunch to reach his century against the spin of Sobers and Gibbs. After Gibbs had taken a wicket in each of his first two overs after lunch, there was a maiden by Gibbs to Engineer, and Engineer reached his century with a single to midwicket in Gibbs' next over. He reached 100 in 143 minutes with 17 fours and was out, for 109, twelve minutes later. With Hall and

Griffith opening, there were only 28 overs bowled before lunch, so scoring 94 off that was a quite remarkable achievement. *The Hindu* newspaper records 44 scoring shots in his 109 (18x4, 2x3, 7x2, 17x1), with no sixes. That paper has a detailed account, but mentions no imbalance in the strike, and it would have taken an extreme imbalance to produce a century in less than 50 balls in that time.

In addition to his 'world record' century, Engineer has persistently claimed both in the two books and in TV interviews that he reached his century with the first ball after lunch, hitting off spinner Lance Gibbs out of the ground for a mighty six. However, neither the report in *The Hindu* nor online scorecards for the match shows him hitting a six in his innings. As Davis notes (and as reported in *The Hindu)*, he got to his ton 23 minutes after lunch, with a single off Lance Gibbs.

Veteran cricket journalist P.N. Sundaresan reported the match for *The Hindu* (14 January 1967), under the byline 'By Our Special Correspondent'. He writes:

Engineer gave a maiden to Gibbs [after lunch] and facing him again, he jumped out to drive a well-flighted delivery but only hit it against his own left-foot. His anxiety and that of the big crowd, waiting to break out into applause, ended when Engineer reached his century with a single to mid-wicket off the next ball. This had taken him only 143 minutes though he had to fight hard for 23 minutes to get his six for the mark after lunch.

If any further evidence is needed, it is provided by a 30-minute highlights package released by the Films Division of India and also available on YouTube.

Though in black and white, the footage is crystal clear. It shows Engineer smashing a couple of lusty drives off the bowling of Charlie Griffith, but there is no six first ball after lunch. On the contrary, he appears hobbled by cramps after the break and is in obvious pain as he takes the single off Gibbs to reach three figures.

This footage is mentioned in some detail by author Evans, who watched it and writes with a touch of skepticism: 'Strangely, there is Indian government film footage which indicates that Engineer completed his century with a single...'

He then quotes Engineer: 'The first ball I faced [after lunch] was from Gibbs. I thought to myself, "This is it. It's him or me." I went down the pitch and smashed it straight down the ground for six. The noise in the stadium was incredible.'

The Times of India's famed reporter K.N. Prabhu, who was at the match, also wrote in *Wisden Asia Cricket*:[26] 'The very sparkle of his innings [before lunch] seemed to take something out of the man: Engineer was bothered by cramps and was held fast on 99 till Rohan Kanhai deliberately (or so it seemed) misfielded to allow him to reach his first Test century.'

Cantrell in his book quotes the match report by Dicky Rutnagur from *Wisden Cricketers' Almanack* (1968 edition), which summarized Farokh's innings as 'a brilliant display of controlled hitting' and noted how he 'smashed a six just after the interval to bring up his hundred.'

The first part of the sentence is indeed in the report, but there is no mention of the six. The second sentence simply does not exist in the famed yearbook. Neither the report in *The Hindu* daily, the newspaper's sister publications *Sport & Pastime* weekly (dated 28 January 1967), *Indian Cricket* annual

---

[26]K.N. Prabhu, 'Engineered to Perfection', *Wisden Asia Cricket*, January 2003

1967 (all written by the same Sundaresan), nor Rutnagur in his reports for *Wisden* and *The Cricketer* monthly and Rusi Modi writing in the March 1967 edition of *Playfair Cricket Monthly*, make any mention of Engineer hitting that six off Gibbs or that he reached his century in 46 (or 47 or 48) balls. Prabhu, as quoted earlier, only reiterates what is obvious on the film footage.

Despite all evidence to the contrary, Engineer has continued to stick to his guns over the years, disregarding the film footage and all on-the-spot reports which prove otherwise. He did so again in two interviews which are also available on YouTube.

On the *Walk the Talk* series of interviews conducted by Shekhar Gupta and telecast on NDTV on 28 April 2013,[27] he tells Gupta at 1:16 in the interview that he hit a century in 46 balls. 'You hit a century in 46 balls in those days?' Gupta asks, surprised. 'Yes indeed, which is supposed to be an all-time record.'

At 2:40, Engineer states: 'First ball after lunch an off spinner comes, by the name of Lance Gibbs...went straight out of the stadium, cleared the whole of Chepauk and it's still travelling, they never found the ball.'

In another video interview on cricketworld.com, broadcast on 18 August 2014,[28] Engineer again makes the claim of his century in 46 balls. Here he states that '*Wisden* in their wisdom' did not keep track of balls faced back then 'and don't say it's the fastest, but it is. I have the scorebook which I will show to you later, which it says very clearly that it was scored in 46

---

[27]'Walk the Talk with Farokh Engineer', NDTV, accessed at: https://www.youtube.com/watch?v=FRGmNjgXsuA
[28]'I Scored The Fastest Ever Test Century - Farokh Engineer's Test Memories-Cricket World TV', Cricket World, accessed at: https://www.youtube.com/watch?v=9qiMJYFnTK8

balls on the first morning of a Test match which had never been done before'. Of course, that scorebook does not exist.

In *Sportstar* weekly dated 2 February 2012, he tells V.V. Subrahmanyam: 'I immediately launched into a huge six [off Gibbs] to reach the century. I can still feel as if the ball is still flying. It is a pity that innings never got its due in terms (sic).'

All this unfortunately obscures the fact that it was indeed a sensational century against possibly the finest bowling attack, and cemented his place in the side.

Victory at the Oval

When India won at the Oval in 1971 for the first time in England to seal the series 1-0, it was Engineer who played a stellar role, with scores of 59 and 28 not out. Remarkably, in the first innings he did not hit a single boundary, still a record for the highest Test score in England without a four or six. In the second, just as things were getting tense, he broke the shackles with a series of bold drives.

G.R. Viswanath was sixth man out, with just four runs needed for victory, when all-rounder Syed Abid Ali walked in. Engineer has, over all these years, resented that he did all the hard work but Abid got the glory, and was chaired off by ecstatic Indian supporters. In his *Outlook* column (and in numerous interviews as well), he wrote: 'Abid rushed out, got a top edge and voila, we were home and Abid was a hero, never mind how he got the run'. Except that it was not a top edge, it was a square cut to the boundary and the video footage is freely available.

There is history between the two, as Sunil Gavaskar revealed in his 1976 autobiography *Sunny Days*. They had attacked each other with bats in the dressing room during the match against East Africa in the 1975 World Cup.

Some years back, Engineer announced on TV during a commentary stint that Abid had died of a heart attack. Fortunately, he is still with us in his seventies now, and in an ironic twist in 2016, rumours spread online that Engineer himself had died!

In 2017, Engineer delivered the fifth M.A.K. Pataudi Memorial lecture in Bengaluru, which was laced with gaffes. He claimed to have opened the innings with Gavaskar in a Test match against Sri Lanka: it never happened, as Lanka entered the Test arena in 1982, long after Engineer had played his final Test. He also claimed that he had been chosen for the World XI in England in 1970 and then in Australia in 1971–72—the only Indian to gain this twin distinction—by 'three knights', namely Sir Don Bradman, Sir Len Hutton and Sir Frank Worrell. But Worrell had died in 1967, at the age of 42!

Sadly, despite being made aware of this gaffe, Engineer was at it again at the Dilip Sardesai Memorial Lecture in Mumbai in December 2019. Surely, this is being disrespectful to the memory of a great cricketer.

For decades now, Engineer has been claiming that he was the first Indian cricketer to endorse Brylcreem hair cream, which used to be associated with the glamour boys of world cricket like Denis Compton and Keith Miller. In fact, there were other Indians before him—Vinoo Mankad, G.S. Ramchand and Subhash Gupte. This may appear to be a trifling matter, but it does fit into a pattern of boosting his own image and ego.

The idea behind writing this chapter is not to do a hatchet job on one of my first schoolboy cricket heroes. After all, cricketers have committed much worse acts, including murder!

The idea is to set the record straight on facts and figures that have been distorted or misrepresented over the decades and which, till this day, many consider to be correct. The whole idea of this book after all is to bust long-held myths spread, in this case by the player himself, in a pattern of self-aggrandisement, in which he always emerges the hero. The point is, Engineer's feats and records speak for themselves and need no burnishing. But the record needs to be set straight.

BIBLIOGRAPHY

Books:

Vernon Addison and Brian Bearshaw: Lancashire Cricket at the Top (Stanley Paul); Tom Alter and Ayaz Memon: The Best in the World: India's Ten Greatest World Cup Matches (Penguin Books); Vijay Amritraj: My Autobiography (Rupa Publications India); Khalid Ansari (editor): Wills Book of Cricket: Champions of One-Day Cricket (Orient Longman); James Astill: The Great Tamasha: Cricket, Corruption and the Turbulent Rise of Modern India (Extract used by kind permission of Bloomsbury Publishing Plc; 1st edition, 2013); Rajan Bala: Glimpses at Perfection: The Story of Indian Cricket Technique (Dronequill Publishers); Kausik Bandyopadhyay: Mahatma on the Pitch: Gandhi & Cricket in India: The Story of a Forgotten Partnership (Rupa Publications India); Jack Bannister (compiler): The Innings of My Life (Headline); Benson & Hedges World Championship of Cricket Official Book 1985 (A Playbill Sport Publication, Australia); Scyld Berry: Cricket Wallah: With England in India 1981-82; (Hodder & Stoughton); W.A.

Bettesworth: Chats on the Cricket Field (Merrit & Hatcher Ltd); Soumya Bhattacharya: All That You Can't Leave Behind: Why We Can Never Do Without Cricket (Penguin Books); Soumya Bhattacharya: You Must Like Cricket?: Memoirs of an Indian Cricket Fan (Yellow Jersey Press, Random House); Kishore Bhimani: West Indies '76: India's Caribbean Adventure (Nachiketa Publications Ltd); Henry Blofeld: My A-Z of Cricket: A Personal Celebration of our Glorious Game (Hodder & Stoughton); Derek Birley: The Willow Wand: Some Cricket Myths Explored (Aurum Press Ltd); Dickie Bird: My Autobiography (Hodder & Stoughton); Alan Border: Beyond Ten Thousand: My Life Story (Swan Publishing Ltd); Don Bradman: Farewell to Cricket (Hodder & Stoughton); Mike Brearley: Spirit of Cricket: Reflections on Play and Life (Constable); Gerald Brodribb: Hit for Six (Heinemann); Gerald Brodribb: Next Man In: A Survey of Cricket Laws and Customs (Rupa Publications India); John Cantrell: Farokh Engineer: From the Far Pavilion (Tempus Publishing Ltd); Richard Cashman: Patrons, Players and the Crowd: The Phenomenon of Indian Cricket (Orient Longman Limited); Robert Cardwell: The Tied Test in Madras: Controversy, Courage and Crommo (The Cricket Publishing Company); Greg Chappell: Fierce Focus (Hardie Grant); Mike Coward: Cricket Beyond the Bazaar: Australia on the Indian subcontinent (Allen & Unwin Australia Pty Ltd); Tony Cozier: The West Indies: Fifty Years of Test Cricket (Rupa Publications India); Cricket Alight! World Series Cricket in Australia, New Zealand and the West Indies (Golden Press Pty Ltd in association with World Series Cricket); Cricket Alive! World Series Cricket: The First Exciting Year (Golden Press Pty Ltd in association with World Series Cricket); Cricket in Australia: Ten Turbulent Years: Centenary Test-Bicentenary Test (Swan Publishing Pty Ltd); Antony de Mello:

Portrait of Indian Sport (Macmillan); Kapil Dev: Straight from the Heart: An Autobiography (Macmillan); Anindya Dutta: Wizards: The Story of Indian Spin Bowling (Westland Publications); Colin Evans: Farokh: The Cricketing Cavalier (Max Books); Gulu Ezekiel and Vijay Lokapally: Speed Merchants: The Story of Indian Pace Bowling 1880s to 2019 (Bloomsbury); Forty Years of Sportstar; 40 Superstars (THG Publishing Private Limited); Bill Frindall: Limited-Overs International Cricket: The Complete Record (Headline Book Publishing); The Wisden Book of One-Day Internationals 1971-1985 (Compiled by Bill Frindall and Victor H. Isaacs; John Wisden & Co; 1986 edition. Extract used by kind permission of Bloomsbury Publishing Plc); The Wisden Book of Test Cricket (John Wisden and Co; various editions); Sunil Gavaskar: Idols (Rupa Publications India); One-day Wonders (Rupa Publications India); Runs 'n Ruins (Rupa Publications India); Sunny Days (Rupa Publications India); Chris Gayle: Six Machine: I Don't Like Cricket...I Love it (Viking Penguin); Charlie Griffith: Chucked Around (Pelham); Ramachandra Guha: A Corner of a Foreign Field: The Indian History of a British Sport (Penguin); Ramachandra Guha and T.G. Vaidyanathan (editors): An Indian Cricket Omnibus (Oxford University Press); Michael Holding: No Holding Back: The Autobiography (Orion Books Ltd); Whispering Death: The Life and Times of Michael Holding (with Tony Cozier; Rupa Publications India); Nasser Hussain, Peter Baxter and Mike Brearley: Cricket's Greatest Battles (Generation Publications); Indian Cricket annual (Kasturi & Sons; various); The Indian Cricket Field annual (various); Martin Johnson and Henry Blofeld: The Independent World Cup Cricket '87 (The Kingswood Press); Dean Jones: Deano: My Call (Swan Publishing); Alvin Kallicharran: Colour Blind: Struggles,

Sacrifice and Success of the Cricket Legend (Notion Press. com); Mukul Kesavan: Men in White: A Book of Cricket (Penguin); Prashant Kidambi: Cricket Country: The Untold History of the First All India Team (Penguin Viking/Penguin Random House India); Dennis Lillee: Menace (Headline Book Publishing); Clive Lloyd: Living for Cricket (Stanley Paul); Simon Lister: Fire in Babylon: How the West Indies Cricket Team Brought a People to its Feet (Yellow Jersey Press); Boria Majumdar: Once Upon a Furore: Lost Pages of Indian Cricket (Yoda Press); Devon Malcolm: You Guys Are History! An Autobiography (Willow Publishing); Michael Manley: A History of West Indies Cricket (Andre Deutsch and Pan Books); Kersi Meher-Homji: Six Appeal: On Soaring Sixes and Lusty Hitters (Kangaroo Press); Raju Mukherji: Cricket in India: Origin and Heroes (UBSPD); Nikhil Naz: Miracle Men: The Greatest Underdog Story in Cricket (Hachette India); Omar Noman: Pride and Passion: An Exhilarating Half Century of Cricket in Pakistan (Oxford University Press); Mansur Ali Khan Pataudi: Tiger's Tale: The Story of the Nawab of Pataudi (Stanley Paul & Co Ltd); J.M. Framjee Patel: Stray Thoughts on Indian Cricket (The Marine Sports); Devendra Prabhudesai: SMG: A Biography of Sunil Manohar Gavaskar (Rupa Publications India); Vasant Raiji: India's Hambledon Men (Tyeby Press); C.K. Nayudu: The Shahenshah of Indian Cricket (The Marine Sports); V. Ramnarayan: Third Man: Reflections of a Life in Cricket (Westland Ltd); Sundar Rajan: India v West Indies 1971 (Jaico Books); K.S. Ranjitsinhji: The Jubilee Book of Cricket (William Blackwood and Sons); Mario Rodrigues: Batting for the Empire: A Political History of Ranjitsinhji (Penguin); Peter Roebuck: Sometimes I Forgot to Laugh (Allen & Unwin); Alan Ross: Ranji (Pavilion Books Ltd); PR Man Singh: Victory Insight: A Manager's Diary for the 1983 and 1987 World Cup (The Marine

Sports); Balvinder Singh Sandhu with Austin Coutinho: The Devil's Pack: The Men Behind the '83 Victory (Rupa Publications India); Berry Sarbadhikary: My World of Cricket: A Centenary of Tests (Cricket Library India); Rajdeep Sardesai: Democracy's XI: The Great Indian Cricket Story (Juggernaut); Michael Sexton: Border's Battlers: The Furnace of Madras, the tied Test, a defining Moment for Australian Cricket (Affirm Press); Bob Simpson: Cricket Then and Now (Allen & Unwin); PR Man Singh: Cricket Biryani: The History of Hyderabad Cricket (The Marine Sports); Rick Smith: Great Days in Test Cricket (ABC Books); Garry Sobers: My Autobiography (Headline); Shashi Tharoor and Shaharyar Khan: Shadows Across the Playing Field: 60 Years of India-Pakistan Cricket (Roli Books); Chris Waters: Fred Trueman: The Authorised Biography (Aurum); Sudhir Vaidya: Vinoo Mankad (Thacker & Co. Ltd); Wisden Cricketers' Almanack 1952, 1963, 1972 editions: Norman Preston (editor); 2002 edition: Graeme Wright (editor)—John Wisden & Co. Extracts used by kind permission of Bloomsbury Publishing Plc; Steve Waugh: Out of my Comfort Zone: The Autobiography (Penguin Viking); Simon Wilde: A Genius Rich and Strange (Aurum Press); World Championship of Cricket Limited Edition (Victoria Cricket Association);Tim Zoehrer: The Gloves are Off (EMW Publications); 200 Seasons of Australian Cricket (Pan Macmillan Australia)

Periodicals, newspapers:

Australian Cricket; Back Spin; Anandji Dossa's Cricket Quarterly; Sportstar; Sportsweek; Sportsweek World of Cricket; The Cricketer; National Nine World Champions Guide; The Benson & Hedges World Championship of Cricket guide; Cricketer Asia; Daily Telegraph (Australia); Daily Telegraph

(UK): The Independent; Hindustan Times; Inside Edge; Inside Cricket; Glasgow Herald; The Times of India; The Hindu; The Indian Express; Readers Digest; Sport & Pastime; The Nightwatchman; Playfair Cricket Monthly; Between Wickets; Scores & Biographies; The Sunday Times of India; Wisden Asia Cricket; Cricinfo Monthly; Mid-day; Straight Bat; The Age (Melbourne); Sunday Telegraph (Australia); Sun (Australia); The Truth; The News (Australia); World Cricket Digest; Wisden Cricket Monthly.

Websites

bcci.tv; sportstats.com.au; espncricinfo.com; bbc.com; cricketcountry.com; cricketarchive.com; rediff.com; twitter. com; www.thecricketmonthly.com; www.cricketweb.net; trov. nla.gov.au (for vintage Australian publications)

Documentary/DVD

Madras Magic: The Tied Test of '86 (Australian Broadcasting Corporation); India v West Indies 1966-67 series (Films Division).

ACKNOWLEDGEMENTS

Abbas Ali Baig; Mark Baldwin; S.S. Bhakoo; Sarang Bhalerao; Peter Binns; Nick Bridge; Dhananjaya Chak; Martin Chandler; Saibal Chatterjee; Annie Chave; Mohit Choudhuri; Lawrie Colliver; Mike Coward; Charles Davis; Rick Eyre; David Frith; Mayukh Ghosh; Neil Hunter; Nick Hunter; Novy Kapadia; Murali Kartik; Pratyush Khaitan; K.C.A Vijaya Kumar; Anil Kumble; Kersi Meher-Homji; Suresh Menon; R. Mohan; Raju Mukherji; Seema Mukherji; Navneet Mundhra; Clayton Murzello; Roger Page; Dr Nigel Pyne; N. Ram; V. Ramnarayan; Mark Ray; Neil Robinson; Mario Rodrigues; M. Sankar; Subu Sastry; P.R. Man Singh; Maninder Singh; Mainak Sinha; B. Sreeram; Sankaran Srinivasan; Rob Steen; Bill Stingas; David Studham; Andrew Summerral; Vincent Sunder; Bhaskeran Thomas; Sidhartha Vaidyanathan; Karthik Venkatesh.

INDEX

162, 173, 177, 180, 197